AF600336

THE RENUNCIATION OF AN ECCLESIASTICAL OFFICE

The Catholic University of America
Canon Law Studies
No. 218

THE RENUNCIATION OF AN ECCLESIASTICAL OFFICE

A HISTORICAL SYNOPSIS AND COMMENTARY

BY THE
Rev. Gerald V. McDevitt, S.T.L., J.C.L.
PRIEST OF THE ARCHDIOCESE OF PHILADELPHIA

A DISSERTATION
Submitted to the Faculty of the School of Canon Law of the Catholic University of America in Partial Fulfillment of the Requirements for the Degree of Doctor of Canon Law

THE CATHOLIC UNIVERSITY OF AMERICA PRESS
WASHINGTON, D. C.
1946

Nihil Obstat:
EDUARDUS G. ROELKER, S.T.D., J.C.D.,
Censor Deputatus
Washington, D. C., die 8 maii 1945.

Imprimatur:
✠ D. CARD. DOUGHERTY,
Archiepiscopus Philadelphiensis
Philadelphiae, die 11 maii 1945.

MURRAY & HEISTER—WASHINGTON, D. C.
PRINTED IN THE UNITED STATES

9

To
My Father
and
Mother

TABLE OF CONTENTS

PART TWO

CANONICAL COMMENTARY

FOREWORD

With reference to ecclesiastical offices one is inclined to think almost exclusively of the manner of conferral of such offices and of the qualities required in the subject for the reception of them. Such an attitude tends to give the impression that the Church in her legislation has not given and does not give much attention to the question of how an ecclesiastical office may be forfeited by the incumbent after he has once received it. Any such impression is entirely wrong, for there is an abundance of past and present legislation that gives ample testimony to the Church's care in this regard. It is logical, too, that the Church should exercise such care in this matter, for it is an element that exerts a profound influence on the external rule of the ecclesiastical society.

In the present work a specific mode by which an ecclesiastical office is lost, namely, the renunciation of an office by its incumbent, is under consideration. The renunciation may be either express or tacit. The former type is one that is executed in accordance with the various formalities prescribed in the law; the latter type is one that is effected by the mere placing or omission of certain specific acts to which the law attaches the effect of a renunciation. Both types of renunciation are considered in this work.

It must be emphasized from the beginning that the type of ecclesiastical office that is under consideration here is an ecclesiastical office in the strict sense as it is defined in canon 145, § 1, for the rules in canons 184–191 which regulate the renunciation of an ecclesiastical office apply only to offices in the strict sense. Canon 145, § 2, establishes the presumption that the term "ecclesiastical office," when used in the law, denotes an ecclesiastical office in the strict sense unless the opposite meaning is apparent from the context. There is nothing in the canons which treat of the renunciation of an ecclesiastical office to destroy this presumption.

Likewise, it is important to note that the present work is a treatment of the renunciation of an ecclesiastical office in general. It is not simply a treatment of the renunciation of an ecclesiastical benefice, which is a specific type of ecclesiastical office. While it is true that the legislation on ecclesiastical offices in general applies also to benefices, there are also some special prescriptions with reference to the latter. Such special prescriptions will not receive primary consideration, and the writer will make mention of benefices only when he believes that such mention is required for the sake of clarity or completeness.

After a short introductory chapter containing necessary preliminary remarks and definitions, the work is divided into two parts, namely, a historical synopsis and a canonical commentary. In the former part an attempt is made to present in a chronological succession within a logical order a general picture of the historical development of the legislation on the renunciation of an ecclesiastical office. In the period prior to the Code of Canon Law the greater part of the legislation had reference to the renunciation of an ecclesiastical benefice, and the indiscriminate use of the terms "office, benefice, dignity and personate," makes it difficult at times to separate the legislation into definite categories. The Code, on the other hand, presents a distinct set of rules for the regulation of the renunciation of an ecclesiastical office in general. In the latter part of this work an attempt is made to present as clearly as possible the proper interpretation of the present-day legislation of the Code of Canon Law.

Since an express renunciation and a tacit renunciation of an ecclesiastical office differ greatly as to the manner of their execution, they receive separate consideration in both parts of this work.

The writer wishes to express his sincere gratitude to His Eminence, Dennis Cardinal Dougherty, Archbishop of Philadelphia, for the opportunity to pursue advanced studies at the Catholic University of America, and to the members of the Faculty of the School of Canon Law for their profitable instruction and kind assistance.

CHAPTER I

PRELIMINARY REMARKS

Article I. The Definition of an Ecclesiastical Office

The concept of an ecclesiastical office has varied somewhat in the history of the Church. The purpose of an ecclesiastical office has always been that of aiding the Church in the attainment of her end, namely, the eternal salvation of men. Jesus Christ established a double hierarchy of orders and of jurisdiction for the Church, but the Church had to add to the nucleus by the creation of other offices which participated in and aided the divinely instituted hierarchy in the completion of its task. In practice it was difficult to determine in what way and to what extent a definite charge had to participate in this work of the Church in order to be classified as an ecclesiastical office in the strict sense of the term.

Prior to the Code of Canon Law an ecclesiastical office in the strict sense was restricted in its application to those incumbencies which participated in the power of jurisdiction. Hence Wernz (1842–1914) defined an office in the strict sense as follows:

> *. . . est gradus quidam jurisdictionis ecclesiasticae quoad personas, causas, locum legibus Christi vel Ecclesiae in perpetuum ita institutus, ut jura et onera spiritualia ipsi adnexa nomine proprio et ratione quadam stabili sint exercenda.*[1]

While a grade of jurisdiction was necessary to constitute an office in the strict sense, all that was necessary to constitute an office in the broad sense was that the charge have annexed to it the right of performing some act of orders or of administering ecclesiastical things.[2]

---

[1] *Ius Decretalium* (6 vols., Vol. II, 3. ed., 1915, Prati), II, n. 240.

[2] Wernz, *loc. cit.*

The Code, retaining for the concept of an ecclesiastical office the essential elements predicated for it in the pre-Code law, extended the definition of an office whether taken in a strict sense or understood in a broad conception of that term. The Code defines an ecclesiastical office in the broad sense as ". . . *quodlibet munus quod in finem spiritualem legitime exercetur.*" [3] Hence the only requisite for an office in the broad sense is that it be a charge which is exercised according to the norms of law for the glory of God and the good of souls. According to this definition an organist, a sacristan and other like persons must be considered to have an office in the broad sense. It is worthy of note also that the incumbent of an office in the broad sense may be a lay person, since there is no power of jurisdiction or of orders necessarily involved in such an office.

The definition of an ecclesiastical office in the strict sense demands closer attention and examination, for the present work deals precisely with the renunciation of offices which can and must be considered as such in the strict sense. The definition of an ecclesiastical office in the strict sense, as given by the Code, reads as follows:

> . . . *munus ordinatione sive divina sive ecclesiastica stabiliter constitutum ad normam sacrorum canonum conferendum, aliquam saltem secumferens participationem ecclesiasticae potestatis sive ordinis sive iurisdictionis.*[4]

As is evident from the definition itself, the concept of an ecclesiastical office in the strict sense has been widened to include also the case of a participation in the power of orders as a sufficient foundation for such an office.

There are four constitutive elements in the definition of an office in the strict sense: [5]

a—Divine or ecclesiastical institution—This requirement auto-

---

[3] Can. 145, § 1.

[4] Can. 145, § 1.

[5] Cocchi, *Commentarium in Codicem Iuris Canonici* (8 vols., Vol. II, 4. ed., 1937; Vol. VIII, 4. ed., 1938, Taurinorum Augustae: Marietti), II, n. 59. Hereafter this work is cited as *Commentarium.*

matically excludes the State from any competency in the establishment of an ecclesiastical office. Some offices, as, for example, the papacy and the episcopate, have been established by divine institution; others, like the offices of the metropolitan and of the vicar general, are of ecclesiastical origin. Maroto (1875–1937) makes a distinction between the institution of an office *in genere* and *in specie.*[6] An example will best explain what he means by this distinction. The episcopate has been established by Christ as an office for the universal Church. That is the constitution of the office *in genere.* The individual bishoprics are constituted by the Roman Pontiff. This is the constitution *in specie.*

b—Stability—This property of an office demands that a position, once established by the competent authority, remain in existence independently of his will and of the will of the incumbent. All authors agree that this stability is an objective stability, that is, that it applies to the office itself and not to the incumbent's tenure of office.[7] This objective stability does not require that the office be transferred from incumbent to incumbent without interruption. All that is necessary is that it be conferred when the circumstances demanding it are verified, as, for example, is the case with reference to the office of the vicar capitular.[8] McBride expresses this point well by saying that the stability has reference to the constitution of the office *in genere* and not to its constitution *in specie.*[9]

c—Conferral according to the canons—The prescriptions of

[6] *Institutiones Iuris Canonici* (2 vols., Vol. I, 3. ed., 1921, Romae: Apud Commentarium pro Religiosis), I, n. 582. Hereafter this work is cited as *Institutiones.*

[7] Blat, *Commentarium Textus Codicis Iuris Canonici* (5 vols. in 6, Vol. II, 2. ed., 1921; Vol. III, Pars altera, 1923, Romae: F. Ferrari), II, n. 85 (Hereafter this work is cited as *Commentarium*); Vermeersch-Creusen, *Epitome Iuris Canonici* (3 vols., Vol. I, 6. ed., 1937; Vol. III, 5. ed., 1936, Mechlinae-Romae: H. Dessain), I, n. 263 (Hereafter this work cited as *Epitome*); Maroto, *Institutiones,* I, n. 579.

[8] Wernz-Vidal, *Ius Canonicum* (7 vols. in 8, Vol. II, 2. ed., 1928, Romae: Apud Aedes Universitatis Gregorianae), II, n. 140; Vermeersch-Creusen, *Epitome,* I, n. 227.

[9] *Incardination and Excardination of Seculars,* The Catholic University of America Canon Law Studies, n. 145 (Washington, D. C.: The Catholic University of America Press, 1941), p. 431.

canon law must be followed in the making of appointments to ecclesiastical offices, for in their existence these offices depend, not on the will of the appointing superior, but on the law of the Church. Maroto claims that this prescription holds even with reference to an office established by particular law.[10]

d—Possession of some participation in the powers of orders or of jurisdiction—The statement of the canon in this matter is quite general, and as a result controversies have arisen in the determination of its precise meaning.

With reference to the participation in the power of orders Vidal (1867–1938) states that the power attached to the office must be a power over and above that which the incumbent obtained at the time of his ordination.[11] Cocchi,[12] Claeys Bouuaert-Simenon [13] and McBride [14] accept the power of orders received at the time of ordination as sufficient to satisfy the requirements of the definition of an office in the strict sense. Coronata [15] and Maroto [16] go still a step further. They state that the recitation of the divine office and other like functions imply a sufficient participation in the power of orders to furnish a basis in this particular regard for the constituting of an office in the strict sense.

McBride explains rather clearly his opinion in this matter. He states that the power of orders must be a power of orders in the strict sense of the term. Hence he excludes the recitation of the divine office and other similar functions. He admits that the power of orders attached to an office may be one that is special and distinct from that acquired in ordination, but he does not require that it be such in order to satisfy the requirement of the participation in the power of orders in an office in the

[10] *Institutiones,* I, p. 675, footnote 3.

[11] *Ius Canonicum,* II, n. 140.

[12] *Commentarium,* II, n. 59.

[13] *Manuale Juris Canonici* (3 vols., Vol. I, 3. ed., 1930, Gandae et Leodii: Seminarium Gandavense et Leodiense) I, n. 306. Hereafter this work is cited as *Manuale.*

[14] *Incardination and Excardination of Seculars,* p. 435.

[15] *Institutiones Iuris Canonici* (5 vols., Vol. I, 1928; Vol. IV, 1935, Taurini: Marietti), I, n. 204. Hereafter this work is cited as *Institutiones.*

[16] *Institutiones,* I, n. 579.

strict sense. The power of orders already acquired by ordination is sufficient, provided that the office carries with it the right to exercise that power within a given sphere. Thus, the office of a coadjutor bishop contains in it the right to exercise pontifical orders, with the exception of ordinations, in the territory of the diocese, and is therefore an office in the strict sense. In this sense, according to McBride, the power of orders acquired at the time of ordination is sufficient to constitute the requisite element of the participation in the power of orders in an ecclesiastical office in the strict sense.

The same type of difficulty is encountered in the determination of the power of jurisdiction which is necessary as an element for constituting an office in the strict sense. While it is readily admitted by the authors that this power may pertain either to the internal forum or to the external forum, it is not so readily admitted that this power may be either ordinary power or delegated power. The majority of the authors seems to take it for granted that ordinary power is required to constitute an office in the strict sense.[17] Presumably they arrive at this conclusion because of the fact that the Code defines ordinary power as that which is by law attached to an office.[18]

Vermeersch-Creusen,[19] Sipos[20] and McBride,[21] on the contrary, maintain that it is possible to have an ecclesiastical office in the strict sense with only delegated power as its content. Sipos contends that the definition of ordinary power as that power which is attached to an office *ipso iure* does not warrant the conclusion that every office must have ordinary power. The superior could attach delegated power to an office, as, for example, in the case of synodal judges, and this delegated power would be sufficient to constitute it an office in the strict sense, provided that the other requirements were present. McBride maintains that the

[17] Cf. Wernz-Vidal, *Ius Canonicum,* II, n. 140; Maroto, *Institutiones,* I, n. 579; Coronata, *Institutiones,* I, n. 278.

[18] Can. 197, § 1.

[19] *Epitome,* II, n. 742.

[20] "Ad officium sacrum an requiritur potestas ordinaria"—*Ius Pontificium* (Romae, 1921-), XVI (1936), 67.

[21] *Incardination and Excardination of Seculars,* p. 446.

requirement of the law on this point is satisfied as long as the office has attached to it the efficacious right that some power be delegated to the incumbent of each specific office by the proper superior.

Hilling takes exception to the arguments of Sipos and defends the more common opinion which holds that "office" and "ordinary power" are correlative terms.[22] He admits that the definition of an office which the Code gives does not make this point clear, but he maintains that it becomes quite clear when the definition of an office is compared with the definition of ordinary power. Ordinary power is something inherent in the office; delegated power is merely complementary. Since synodal judges have only delegated powers, Hilling denies that they have an office in the strict sense. To his mind their nomination is merely a recognition of their qualities and ability, and does not carry with it any participation in the power of jurisdiction. They receive their jurisdiction when they are commissioned for specific cases.

This discussion could be carried on at great length. The intention of the writer was to give a brief glance at the two opinions with their underlying arguments without attempting to solve the problem involved. The writer favors the opinion which holds that ordinary power is necessary as an element for the constituting of an office in the strict sense. In spite of some difficulties that such an opinion creates, it seems, nevertheless, to be the opinion which harmonizes more intimately with the concept of ordinary and delegated power as presented in the Code.

Article II. The Definition of an Ecclesiastical Benefice

Although the present work is not a treatise on the renunciation of an ecclesiastical benefice, which is a particular type of ecclesiastical office, nevertheless, since the close relationship of these two institutes will demand that benefices receive some consideration at times, a brief explanation of the definition of a benefice is presented here. The close relationship of these two institutes is clearly shown in the Code where it states that the

[22] "Kirchliches *Officium* und *Potestas ordinaria*"—*Archiv für katholisches Kirchenrecht* (Innsbruck, 1857-1861; Mainz, 1862-), CXVII (1937), 433. Hereafter this periodical is cited as *AKKR*.

laws on ecclesiastical offices apply to benefices as well.[23]

Canon 1409 defines an ecclesiastical benefice as follows:

> . . . *est ens iuridicum a competente ecclesiastica auctoritate in perpetuum constitutum seu erectum, constans officio sacro et iure percipiendi reditus ex dote officio adnexos.*

This definition declares a benefice to be a moral person consisting of two elements, namely, a sacred office and the right to receive from the endowment the revenue attached to the office.

a—The benefice is a moral person—This means that it is by law considered a subject of rights and obligations. The benefice is a non-collegiate moral person composed, therefore, not of physical persons, but of the sacred office and the right to the revenue attached to the office.[24]

b—The benefice must contain a sacred office—The benefice is in fact a species of ecclesiastical office. Whatever is predicated of offices in general may be applied to benefices also, but the converse is not true.[25] As has already been noted, there are two types of ecclesiastical office, namely, the ecclesiastical office in the broad sense and in the strict sense. The ecclesiastical office which is required in order to be constituted as a benefice is an ecclesiastical office in the strict sense. The Code establishes the presumption that the term "ecclesiastical office" must be interpreted to mean an ecclesiastical office in the strict sense unless the opposite meaning is apparent from the context.[26] Since there is nothing in the context of canon 1409 to destroy this presumption, the benefice must contain an office in the strict sense.[27]

c—The benefice must contain the right to receive from the endowment the revenue attached to the office—Under the present law the concept of the endowment has been extended in its meaning to include many sources of revenue. The Code permits the

---

[23] Can. 146.

[24] Haydt, *Reserved Benefices,* The Catholic University of America Canon Law Studies, n. 161 (Washington, D. C.: The Catholic University of America Press, 1942), p. 62.

[25] Coronata, *Institutiones,* I, n. 205.

[26] Can. 145, § 2.

[27] Haydt, *Reserved Benefices,* p. 66.

endowment to be constituted by property owned by the benefice itself as a moral person, by contributions whose payment is imposed upon families or corporations, by reliable voluntary offerings of the faithful, by stole fees regulated by the diocesan statutes or by legitimate custom, or by choral distributions, excepting, however, one-third part of the last mentioned distributions if the entire revenue of the benefice is made up of such distributions.[28] Besides, if the benefice is a parochial benefice, a dowry in one of the above-mentioned senses is not necessary, provided that the superior prudently foresees that sufficient income will not be lacking.[29]

Article III. The Definition of a Renunciation of an Ecclesiastical Office

The Code enumerates five different ways by which an ecclesiastical office may be lost by the incumbent.[30] First mention is given by the Code to the way that is under consideration in the present work, namely, the renunciation of the office by the incumbent.

Before the Code of Canon Law a distinction was made between the terms " renunciation " and " resignation " with reference to ecclesiastical offices. The latter term was used to designate a special type of renunciation, namely, one that was made in favor of another person.[31] The Code has given no recognition to this distinction and makes use of the two terms as synonyms.[32] The Code does, however, make exclusive use of the term *dimissio,* to designate the renunciation of a benefice.[33]

The Code does not provide a definition of the renunciation of an office. Maroto, gathering the elements from the canons which treat of the renunciation of an office, describes it as follows:

> *Libera cessio officii ecclesiastici, ex iusta causa, apud competentem superiorem ecclesiasticum facta et ab ipso acceptata.*[34]

[28] Can. 1410.

[29] Can. 1415, § 3.

[30] Can. 183, § 1.

[31] Wernz, *Ius Decretalium,* II, n. 493, footnote 3.

[32] Cf. Can. 157; 2400.

[33] Maroto, *Institutiones,* I, p. 804, footnote 2.

[34] *Ibid.,* n. 678.

Since the elements of this definition will be considered in detail in the commentary section of this work, it is not necessary to subject them to analysis here. It is sufficient to note the various types of renunciation of office. The renunciation of an office may be express or tacit. The former type is one which is made in accordance with all the solemnities prescribed in the law. The latter, on the other hand, is one that is contained in an act or omission, imputable to the incumbent, to which the law attaches the effect of a resignation. No solemnities are required. It suffices that the incumbent be accountable for the act or omission to which the law attaches the effect of a tacit renunciation. The vacancy follows immediately without the need of any declaration on the part of the superior. Canon 188 contains an all-inclusive list of the acts and omissions which beget a tacit renunciation of office.

Express renunciation of office may be either absolute or conditional. An absolute resignation is one that is made unqualified by any agreement or condition; a conditional one rests upon some kind of proviso or is bound up with some kind of agreement which must be fulfilled if it is to become effective. The latter type is rare, but there are some instances in which the law permits such resignations.[35]

It is to be noted here that the subject under discussion in the present work is the renunciation of a strictly considered ecclesiastical office regarding which the resigning party has a *ius in re*. If a person has a *ius ad rem* by reason of nomination, presentation or election, he may indeed renounce that right, but such a renunciation is not a true renunciation of office, nor is it regulated by the rules which govern the renunciation of an ecclesiastical office.[36] Coronata demands too much, however, when he states that possession of the office along with the *ius in re* is required before the renunciation of the office can be considered a true renunciation.[37] It is true that the taking of possession of an office is often required before one may exercise the jurisdiction attached to the office, as, for example, in the

[35] Cf. Can. 1486–1488.

[36] Coronata, *Institutiones,* I, n. 259.

[37] *Loc. cit.*

case of a bishop,[38] but the title is possessed prior to the fact whereby possession is taken of the office, and hence a renunciation of that right would constitute a true renunciation. This opinion seems to be amply proved by the fact that the Code enumerates among the tacit renunciations in canon 188 the failure to take possession of one's office within the prescribed time.[39]

[38] Can. 334, § 2.

[39] Can. 188, n. 2.

PART ONE

HISTORICAL SYNOPSIS

CHAPTER II

THE DOCTRINE ON EXPRESS RENUNCIATION FROM THE DECREE OF GRATIAN TO THE COUNCIL OF TRENT

ARTICLE I. THE SUBJECT AND OBJECT OF AN EXPRESS RENUNCIATION

In general it may be stated that in this period all persons were capable of renouncing any ecclesiastical office to which they had a *ius in re.* To this general rule, however, there were some exceptions by reason of particular prohibitions which were incorporated into the law. This article will attempt to outline these prohibitions.

SECTION 1. SUBJECTS WHO WERE EXCLUDED FROM RENOUNCING AN OFFICE

A—The Mentally Incapable

In his comments on a letter of Pope Alexander II (1061–1073) the Glossator remarked that the renunciation of a benefice which was involved in the case under consideration would have been valid if it had been made in the hands of the proper superior, provided that the resigning party was *compos sui* at the time.[1] Thus the Glossator required that the person be in possession of his faculties in order to renounce a benefice. For proof of this opinion he made reference to a letter written by Pope Innocent III in the year 1198.[2] In this letter the Pontiff declared that the

[1] *Glossa Ordinaria,* ad c. 1, C. XVIII, q. 2, s.v. *refutavit.*

[2] C. 3, X, *de successione ab intestato,* III, 27; Potthast, *Regesta Pontificum Romanorum inde ab anno post Christum natum MCXCVIII ad annum MCCCIV* (2 vols., Berolini, 1874–1875), n. 252. Hereafter this work is cited as Potthast.

last testament of a certain archbishop would not be sustained if it could be proved that he was not in possession of his faculties at the time he made it.

B—Minors

Minors were excluded from the possibility of renouncing an office without the intervention of a tutor. Pope Alexander III (1159–1181) in a letter to the Archbishop of Canterbury declared that a minor could not administer a church personally, even though one had been conferred upon him by means of a dispensation.[3] The *Glossa Ordinaria* noted that a minor could not have the free administration of anything until he had reached the age of twenty-five years.[4]

Pope Boniface VIII (1294–1303) mitigated this rule when he declared that a minor above the age of puberty could act for himself in regard to spiritual things and anything depending on them.[5] Thus only children below the age of fourteen were prohibited from renouncing an office on their own authority.

SECTION 2. A TYPE OF BENEFICE THAT COULD NOT BE RENOUNCED

The only restriction in this regard in the *Corpus Iuris Canonici* seems to have been the prohibition of renouncing a benefice in favor of a third party when the present incumbent was at court with another regarding his legal right to the benefice. This regulation is contained in a letter of Pope Boniface VIII.[6] The contest had to be settled before the benefice could be conferred upon any one other than the party involved in the dispute.

---

[3] C. 2, X, *de aetate et qualitate et ordine praeficiendorum,* I, 14; Jaffé, *Regesta Pontificum Romanorum ab condita Ecclesia ad annum post Christum natum MCXCVIII* (ed. 2, correctam et auctam auspiciis Gulielmi Wattenbach curaverunt S. Loewenfeld, F. Kaltenbrunner, P. Ewald, 2 vols. in 1, 1885–1888), n. 13808. Hereafter this work is cited as Jaffé.

[4] *Glos. Ord.* ad c. 2, X, *de aetate et qualitate et ordine praeficiendorum,* I, 14, s.v. *aetatem.*

[5] C. 3, *de iudiciis,* II, 1, in VI°.

[6] C. 2, *ut lite pendente nil innovetur,* II, 2, in VI°.

Article II. The Competent Superior for the Admission of an Express Renunciation

Of all the matter contained in the *Corpus Iuris Canonici* on the express renunciation of an office, the greater part has reference to the superior who is competent to receive the resignation. On the whole the legislation is clear, although there are some difficulties involved in the interpretation of it. It is but proper to note in advance that the Roman Pontiff was exempt from the law which demanded that a renunciation of office be made to the competent superior. This question arose during the reign of Pope Boniface VIII, whose predecessor, Celestine V (1294), had renounced the papacy. Boniface VIII in a decretal letter written between the years 1294 and 1298 declared that the Pope could renounce his papal office without obtaining any permission whatsoever.[7]

The *Glossa Ordinaria* of Ioannes Andreae (1272–1348) stated that the Pope could freely resign even if he was sufficiently capable of fulfilling the duties of his office.[8] The reason that the Glossator gave for the total exemption of the Pope in this matter was the fact that the Pope had no superior on earth in whose hands he might renounce his office.[9] Hence in this article the consideration of the legislation will be restricted in its application to those ecclesiastics who are inferior to the Roman Pontiff in station and office. The Roman Pontiff will be spoken of only in so far as he is the competent superior for receiving certain resignations.

Before one presents the legislation which points to the important individual superiors, one may well outline the remarks of the glossators which indicate in a general way the superior to whom the power of receiving resignations pertained. The *Glossa Ordinaria* to a letter of Pope Honorius III (1224) expressed the opinion that a resignation was to be made in the hands of the superior who had the power of confirming the appointment to the office under consideration.[10] A gloss of

[7] C. 1, *de renuntiatione*, I, 7, in VI°.

[8] *Glos. Ord.* ad c. 1, *de renuntiatione*, I, 7, in VI°, s.v. *maxime*.

[9] *Glos. Ord.* ad c. 1, *de renuntiatione*, I, 7, in VI°, s.v. *videbantur*.

[10] *Glos. Ord.* ad c. 15, X, *de renuntiatione*, I, 9, s.v. *in manibus eorundem*.

Ioannes Andreae to a decree of Clement V (1305–1314) in the Council of Vienne (1311–1312) considered as a competent superior anyone who could confer the office or who had the power of confirming the appointment. It concluded, though, by expressing the opinion that perhaps a renunciation of office had to be made in the hands of the superior who had the power of removing the incumbent from the office.[11] An *Additio* to the gloss on the same decree of Clement V remarked that if someone had the right of election or presentation to the office, his consent also had to be obtained when a renunciation of the office was accepted.[12]

These remarks were deductions of the Glossators which served to indicate, although obscurely, the general scheme that was followed in the determination of the competent superior. No decree or law set this down as a rule. The laws had reference to the specific superior in individual cases. The three more important competent superiors will now be considered.

SECTION 1. THE ROMAN PONTIFF

A pseudo-Isidorian letter attributed to Pope Evaristus (99?–107?) stated that a bishop was not to give up his church except in a case of inevitable necessity or in virtue of the authority of the Holy See.[13] The *Glossa Ordinaria* of Ioannes Teutonicus (+1245) noted that this letter spoke of a bishop who abandoned his own see in order that he might attach himself to another one.[14] Nevertheless this letter served to bring out in a general way the idea that the authority of the Holy See was required in order that a bishop might renounce his office.

Later, Pope Nicholas I (858–867) issued a letter in which he declared that a certain Suffredus should be restored to his see since he did not refer his case to the proper authority for judgment.[15] The letter itself is not particularly relevant, but the remarks of the Glossator are very much to the point. From the

[11] *Glos. Ord.* ad c. un, *de renuntiatione,* I, 4, in Clem., s.v. *manibus.*
[12] *Additio* ad c. un., *de renuntiatione,* I, 4, in Clem., s.v. *manibus.*
[13] C. 11, C. VII, q. 1; Jaffé, n. †21.
[14] *Glos. Ord.* ad c. II, C. VII, q. 1, s.v. *dimittere.*
[15] C. 3, C. VI, q. 1; Jaffé, n. 2791.

fact that the Pope restored the bishop to his see the Glossator deduced that a renunciation was not valid if made without the superior's knowledge or in the hands of another. Against this deduction he raised the argument that there was a tacit renunciation in such cases. Finally, he solved the difficulty by saying that such a resignation held as far as the resigning party was concerned, but the Church could recall him to office again, as was done by the Pope in this case.[16] The question of the validity of such a resignation will be treated later. The remarks of the Glossator are cited here merely to show the necessity of making a resignation to the proper superior, in this instance to the Pope.

Innocent III in the year 1199 explained the reason in consequence of which a bishop could not renounce his see without the permission and authority of the Roman Pontiff. He claimed that the dissolution of the spiritual espousal between a bishop and his see was effected in virtue of a divine rather than a human power, and therefore the Pope, the Vicar of Christ on earth, alone could effect it.[17] The same Pontiff in the year 1208 issued a letter proscribing any custom that derogated from the rule which required the permission of the competent superior when one wished to renounce his office.[18]

Honorius III (1216–1227) in a letter written in the year 1224 declared that the Pope was the competent superior for receiving the renunciation of an exempt abbot.[19] Finally, Hostiensis (+1271), in commenting on a letter of Alexander III, stated that both bishops and exempt abbots had to obtain the permission of the Pope in order to resign and that they had to resign their office in his hands.[20]

SECTION 2. THE BISHOP

Just as the Roman Pontiff was the competent superior for receiving the resignations of bishops and exempt abbots, so did

[16] *Glos. Ord.* ad c. 3, C. VI, q. 3, s.v. *restituatur.*

[17] C. 2, X, *de translatione episcopi,* I, 7; Potthast, n. 575.

[18] C. 7, X, *de consuetudine,* I, 4; Potthast, n. 3397.

[19] C. 15, X, *de renuntiatione,* I, 9; Potthast, n. 7719.

[20] Hostiensis (Henricus de Segusiò), *Commentaria in Quinque Decretalium Libros* (5 vols. in 3, Venetiis, 1581), in c. 4, X, *de renuntiatione,* I, 9, n. 9. Hereafter this work will be cited *Commentaria.*

the bishop stand in that capacity for those under his jurisdiction. There is not so much legislation extant regarding the resignations of lower clerics as there is for the resignations of bishops, but along with the remarks of the Glossators and Commentators there is enough to show that lower clerics also had to abide by a definite rule in this matter.

Pope Alexander III in a letter to the Bishop of Tournai made reference to all benefices under the bishop's jurisdiction, and stated that the consent of the bishop was necessary in order that one might renounce any such benefice.[21] Hostiensis in his commentary on this letter clearly stated that lower clerics as well as non-exempt ones looked for their competent superior to the head of the diocese.[22]

As has already been seen in the preceding section, Innocent III reprobated any custom that allowed one to resign without the permission of the competent superior.[23] The Glossator on Pope Innocent's decretal remarked that an abbot subject to the bishop needed the bishop's permission to renounce his office just as did all other clerics under the bishop's jurisdiction.[24]

SECTION 3. THE LEGATE *a latere*

Among the competent superiors in the matter of accepting a renunciation of office mention must be made of the legates *a latere,* cardinals who represented the Pope in various territories. There is not much legislation in their regard, but there is sufficient to show that they had some authority in this matter, although it is difficult to determine the actual extent of their power.

Innocent IV (1243–1254) issued a letter in which he declared that cardinal legates had the power of conferring benefices in their territory.[25] This letter, it is true, said nothing about the receiving of renunciations from office, but the power of con-

---

[21] C. 4, X, *de renuntiatione,* I, 9; Jaffé, n. 14116.

[22] *Commentaria,* in c. 4, X, *de renuntiatione,* I. 9.

[23] C. 7, X, *de consuetudine,* I, 4; Potthast, n. 3397.

[24] *Glos. Ord.* ad c. 7, X, *de consuetudine,* I, 4, s.v. *migrasse.*

[25] C. 1, *de officio legati,* I, 15, in VI°; Potthast, n. 15121.

ferring offices usually carried with it the right also to receive the resignation.

Boniface VIII in a later decretal letter prohibited a legate from subdelegating his power for the receiving of the renunciation of a benefice.[26] This letter shows clearly that the legate had the power to receive the renunciation of at least some type of benefice. Again Boniface VIII referred to the power of a legate *a latere* in this matter. In another decretal letter he stated that an exempt abbot who was elected to be a bishop could not leave his monastery and take possession of his see without the permission of either the Pope or the legate *a latere*. He likewise stated that such legates had the power to confirm the elections of archbishops, bishops and exempt persons.[27] The *Glossa Ordinaria* noted that what was said of an exempt abbot applied also to any other prelate inferior to a bishop.[28] It stated also that this applied even when the abbot or other prelate was elected to some dignity other than the episcopacy.[29]

While it is difficult to determine the extent of the power of the legate *a latere* in this matter, it is clear that he did have some power. It seems that his power was almost co-extensive with that of the Pope, but there is no proof that he could receive the resignations of bishops. The law merely stated that he could confirm their elections; and although the one who had the power to confirm an appointment to an office usually had also the power to accept the resignation from that office, the latter power was not necessarily implied for the legate, since his power to confirm an appointment was a special power granted to cardinal legates by the Pope. In ultimate analysis the answer to the question could be found only through an investigation of the letter in which the powers were delegated by the Pope.

---

[26] C. 4, *de officio legati,* I, 15, in VI°.

[27] C. 36, *de electione et electi potestate,* I, 6, in VI°.

[28] *Glos. Ord.* ad c. 36, *de electione et electi potestate,* I, 6, in VI°, s.v. *abbatem.*

[29] *Glos. Ord.* ad c. 36, *de electione et electi potestate,* I, 6, in VI°, s.v. *Episcopum.*

SECTION 4. THE VALIDITY OF RESIGNATIONS MADE WITHOUT THE INTERVENTION OF THE COMPETENT SUPERIOR

The previous sections of this article have demonstrated the necessity of making the renunciation of an office in the hands of the competent superior. The question now arises concerning the validity of a resignation made contrary to such a rule.

The Glossator of a letter of Pope Nicholas I offered a solution to the effect that a renunciation of office made without the superior's knowledge or in the hands of another was valid as far as the one resigning was concerned, but that it did not bind the Church to recognize it as such.[30] In other words, the Church could ignore the resignation and restore the person to his office, but the individual himself could not vindicate any claim to the office.

In a letter to the Bishop of Tournai Alexander III invoked a canonical penalty against clerics who renounced their office without their bishop's permission, but he did not state just what the canonical penalty was.[31] Innocent III in the year 1198 declared that a resignation made in the hands of the laity was invalid, but that nevertheless the offender should be deprived of his benefice by way of punishment.[32] The Glossator on this letter remarked that the renunciation held as far as the former incumbent was concerned, but gave the Church or the superior the option of recalling the person to the office.[33] Hostiensis took exception to this view of the Glossator. He maintained that the resignation was considered as invalid by the decretal apart from all distinctions. The incumbent lost the benefice only by privation.[34]

Honorius III, writing to the Bishops of Agde and Nice, decreed that the renunciation of an exempt abbot was null if made without the Pope's permission.[35] Once again the Glossator invoked the opinion that the resignation held only to the prejudice

---

[30] *Glos. Ord.* ad c. 3, C. VI, q. 3, s.v. *restituatur.*

[31] C. 4, X, *de renuntiatione,* I, 9; Jaffé, n. 14116.

[32] C. 8, X, *de renuntiatione,* I, 9; Potthast, n. 390.

[33] *Glos. Ord.* ad c. 8, X, *de renuntiatione,* I, 9, s.v. *in manum laicam resignantes.*

[34] *Commentaria* in c. 8, X, *de renuntiatione,* I, 9, n. 1.

[35] C. 15, X, *de renuntiatione,* I, 9; Potthast, n. 7719.

of the one who resigned in that fashion, and hence he could not attempt to reclaim his benefice or office.[36] On the other hand, Hostiensis taught that the abbot could be forced to renounce his office afterwards, since he was guilty of attempting to renounce it in the hands of one other than the competent superior.[37] St. Raymond of Pennafort (1175–1275) shared the opinion of the Glossator, and stated that the resignation held as far as the one renouncing the benefice was concerned, but that the Church could recall him to the benefice.[38]

The decretal letters themselves seem quite clear in stating that a renunciation of office made in this manner was invalid. In punishment for this violation of the law deprivation of the office was recommended. The opinions of the Glossators and Commentators offer some difficulty. As has been seen, some of them contended that the resignation was valid as far as the person resigning was concerned. This view probably arose from a consideration of the contractual element which was present even when the resignation was made contrary to the law. Thus, these authors held that the one resigning had to observe his part of the contract, namely, the renunciation of the office, even though the resignation itself was invalid.

Before this article is brought to a close, it may be of interest to note that during the early 13th century a person had to complete his resignation once he had obtained the proper permission to renounce his office. It is not clear whether this permission of the superior was the same as the superior's act of acceptance of the resignation, or whether it was something preliminary to the resignation. Innocent III in the IV General Council of the Lateran (1215) was the one who promulgated this rule.[39]

The Glossator explained the reason for this law by saying that the ruling was made to preclude the possibility of any ridicul-

---

[36] *Glos. Ord.* ad c. 15, X, *de renuntiatione,* I, 9, s.v. *in manibus eorundem.*

[37] *Commentaria* in c. 15, X, *de renuntiatione,* I, 9, n. 2.

[38] *Summa* (Veronae, 1744), tit. XXVI, par. 3.

[39] C. 12, X, *de renuntiatione,* I, 9; Mansi, *Sacrorum Conciliorum Nova et Amplissima Collectio* (53 vols. in 60, Paris-Arnhem-Leipzig, 1901–1927), XXII, 1015. Hereafter this work is cited as Mansi.

ing of the Pope.[40] Ioannes Andreae extended the same rule to the case wherein permission had been obtained from other superiors by lower clerics. He stated that the decree made no mention of restricting the ruling simply to the case in which permission had been obtained from the Pope.[41] Hostiensis remarked that one could repent of his intention to resign if he did so before the request for permission to resign had reached the Pope.[42]

Article III. The Sufficient Cause Required for an Express Renunciation

Since an office is given to a cleric for a reason abstracting from his own convenience, it is natural to expect that he would be required to have a just cause before he would be permitted to renounce it. However, it will be seen that the legislation of the Decretal period took little cognizance of this fact as far as lower clerics were concerned.

Alexander III was the first to discuss the necessity of a cause when a bishop wished to renounce his see. In a decretal letter to the Bishop of London the Pope endeavored to convince the bishop that it would be better for him to remain in office with a coadjutor than to cede his office because of old age.[43] The Glossator noted that old age of itself was not a sufficient reason for justifying the resignation from one's office. The condition of advanced years had to be such as to render one incapable of performing one's duties.[44]

The next mention of this matter followed in a letter of Innocent III to the Archbishop of York (1203).[45] The Archbishop of Ragusa had requested permission from the Pope to renounce his see, alleging the reason that he could not reside with safety in the diocese.[46] The Pope granted the required permission to

[40] *Glos. Ord.* ad c. 12, X, *de renuntiatione,* I, 9, s.v. *compellendos.*

[41] *Additio Ioannis Andreae,* c. 12, X, *de renuntiatione,* I, 9, s.v. *compellendos.*

[42] *Commentaria* in c. 12, X, *de renuntiatione,* I, 9, n. 5.

[43] C. 1, X, *de renuntiatione,* I, 9; Jaffé, n. 14008.

[44] *Glos. Ord.* ad c. 1, X, *de renuntiatione,* I, 9, s.v. *senectus.*

[45] C. 9, X, *de renuntiatione,* I, 9; Potthast, n. 1902.

[46] This letter was sent by the Pope to the Archbishop of York because

the Archbishop of Ragusa. The cause involved in the case was the danger of death. The letter of the Pope, however, does not reveal from what source the danger arose. The Glossator suggested that the danger could have arisen either in consequence of an unfavorable climate or as a result of persecution of deadly enemies.[47]

The same Pontiff in the year 1206 drew up an exhaustive list of the causes which were recognized as sufficient to warrant one to ask permission to renounce his office.[48] Hostiensis emphasized the fact that these causes did not justify one's renunciation of office unless also permission had been rightfully granted. They were set down explicitly as causes which sufficed for one to seek permission from the Pope to renounce one's office.[49] The decretal spoke only of bishops in the enumeration of these causes. St. Raymond maintained that for their application these causes were restricted to the offices of prelatures whose renunciation proved prejudicial to others.[50]

In the Pope's letter there is an enumeration of six causes which were considered as sufficient in this regard. On each of these causes the Pope offered a brief explanatory statement, the substance of which is as follows:

(a) Consciousness of Crime—Not all sins or crimes were included under this category. Only such were included as impeded the execution of one's office even after penance had been performed.

(b) Weakness of Body — This cause could arise from either sickness or old age, but it too had to be of such a nature as to render one incapable of performing one's duties.

---

of the fact that the Archbishop of Ragusa, after leaving his see, had received a benefice in the Archdiocese of York.

[47] *Glos. Ord.* ad c. 9, X, *de renuntiatione,* I, 9, s.v. *morari.*

[48] C. 10, X, *de renuntiatione,* I, 9; Potthast, n. 2698.

[49] *Commentaria* in c. 10, X, *de renuntiatione,* I, 9, n. 5.

[50] *Summa,* tit. XXVI, par. III.

(c) Lack of Knowledge — This cause referred to the knowledge necessary for the fulfillment of the duties of the office.

(d) Malice of the People — This cause was present when the people were so obdurate that the bishop could make no spiritual progress with them.

(e) Grave Scandal — When the scandal could not otherwise be removed, the bishop could ask permission to renounce his see lest he appear to esteem the temporal honor more highly than his eternal salvation.

(f) Irregularity — Here the Pope gave two examples of irregularities which were sufficient causes, namely, successive bigamy and marriage to a widow.

These are the six causes which were recognized as sufficient to justify one to ask permission to renounce his see. Nothing was stated regarding the effect that an insufficiency or lack of a cause would have on the subsequent resignation. Since no mention was made of lower clerics, the causes listed in the decretal were applicable only for cases in which a bishop's renunciation of office was in question.

Article IV. The Freedom Required in an Express Renunciation

Throughout the Decretals an appreciable degree of attention was paid to the effect that force, fear and simony had upon a renunciation of office. This article will attempt to present as clearly as possible the doctrine of this period on these points.

Section 1. Freedom from Force and Fear

It will be noticed quite readily that not all the texts of the law were in accord with one another on this point. The main difficulty lies in determining whether the wording of the laws intended to characterize as invalid, or merely as rescissible, any and every renunciation of office effected under duress and fear.

Alexander III in a letter to the Bishop of Worcester stated that a resignation must be made freely.[51] The Pope used the words "*debent in irritum revocari*" with reference to the things "*quae metu et vi fiunt.*" The *Glossa Ordinaria* in its remarks on this letter stated that a resignation made in such circumstances was indeed valid, but could be rescinded.[52] The above cited letter of Alexander III spoke only of fear with regard to this case, and the Glossator likewise limited his consideration to that element. Hostiensis stated that no mention of force was made, since whatever was done under the influence of fierce violence was considered as having been done under the duress of fear also.[53]

Alexander III issued a second letter in which he stated that a person could be reinstated in his benefice if he was induced to resign it through fear inflicted on him by the laity. This reinstatement was to be effected by means of a rescissory action.[54] In the resignation under consideration in the Pontiff's letter the cleric who resigned through fear had also taken an oath at the time that he would not attempt to reclaim the benefice. The Glossator remarked that this type of oath could be kept without danger to one's eternal salvation, but if the influence of fear in the act of resignation stood proved, then the person who had resigned his office or benefice could call on the superior to rescind the resignation and to restore his office or benefice.[55]

Innocent III in the year 1200 reiterated the doctrine of Alexander III, adding, however, that if the oath had reference only to the act of resignation, and not to any disavowal for the reclaiming of the benefice, then the prospective incumbent could

[51] C. 2, X, *de his quae vi metusque causa fiunt,* I, 40; Jaffé, n. 14131.

[52] *Glos. Ord.* ad c. 2, X, *de his quae vi metusque causa fiunt,* I, 40, s.v. *coactus.*

[53] *Commentaria* in c. 2, X, *de his quae vi metusque causa fiunt,* I, 40, n. 7.

[54] C. 3, X, *de his quae vi metusque causa fiunt,* I, 40; Jaffé, n. 16572.

[55] *Glos. Ord.* ad c. 3, X, *de his quae vi metusque causa fiunt,* I, 40, s.v. *iuramento.*

reclaim the benefice.[56] The Glossator explained that if one had taken an oath to renounce his benefice, then the oath obliged him to renounce it, but the oath did not prevent him in any way from trying to reclaim the benefice.[57]

Alexander III also gave two solutions for cases in which the elements of renunciation and spoliation were involved. These solutions had at least an indirect bearing on the matter here discussed. The first case involved a renunciation of a benefice made by the incumbent at a time when he had already been despoiled of his benefice.[58] The Pope decided in this case that in court the exception of renunciation could not be urged or raised against the party who had been previously despoiled of his benefice. There was a presumption against the voluntary character of the resignation in such circumstances. Panormitanus (1386–1453) stated that the exception of renunciation was not admitted in this case, which was being prosecuted as a possessory action, for the simple reason that the exception of renunciation could have reference only to renunciation, after spoliation, of proprietorship and not that of possession, inasmuch as the cleric could not have renounced his possession at a time when he had already been despoiled of it. For this reason he stated that an exception of renunciation could not be raised against the cleric who was prosecuting his case as a possessory action.[59]

In the second case which the Pontiff solved, the resignation had been made by the cleric before the spoliation took place. Here the Pope decided that the cleric was not to be heard if it was proved that he had freely renounced his benefice before he was despoiled of its possession.[60] Panormitanus remarked that in this case the cleric had already lost not only the proprietor-

[56] C. 4, X, *de his quae vi metusque causa fiunt,* I, 40; Potthast, n. 946.

[57] *Glos. Ord.* ad c. 4, X, *de his quae vi metusque causa fiunt,* I, 40, s.v. *repetendam.*

[58] C. 2, X, *de restitutione spoliatorum,* II, 13; Jaffé, n. 14139.

[59] *Commentaria in Quinque Decretalium Libros* (5 vols. in 7, Venetiis, 1588), in c. 2, X, *de restitutione spoliatorum,* II, 13, n. 8. Hereafter this work cited as *Commentaria.*

[60] C. 3, X, *de restitutione spoliatorum,* II, 13; Jaffé, n. 13984.

ship but also the possession of the benefice by the prior resignation.[61]

Clement V (1305–1314) in the Council of Vienne (1311–1312) made a declaration to the effect that renunciations extorted by others were invalid.[62] The *Glossa Ordinaria* stated that such a resignation was totally invalid,[63] and that the means of extortion used in this case were seizure and retention of the person by the secular powers.[64] Panormitanus understood the means used here as incarceration, and accordingly stated that only this caused a renunciation to be invalid when it was made under the influence of fear. All other types of fear merely left room for the renunciation to be rescinded.[65]

The law of the Decretal period, then, held for the validity of a resignation made under the influence of fear. There was, however, the remedy of a rescissory action. Only if incarceration had been used as a means of fear for extorting the resignation did the act of resignation stand as patently invalid.

SECTION 2. FREEDOM FROM SIMONY

Since simony is something to be abhorred, it is not strange that in the *Corpus Iuris Canonici* legislation was enacted against it in the matter of renunciation of office.

Alexander III in one of his decretal letters stated that a simoniacally procured resignation of a benefice was invalid.[66] Hostiensis expressed the opinion that the Pope could recognize such a simoniacal pact as valid and binding if he so wished, since he had the fulness of power in the Church. With such papal action the resignation could become valid in its juridical effect.[67]

Pope Gregory IX (1227–1241) interdicted in a general way pecuniary agreements in any type of spiritual matters.[68] Finally,

---

[61] *Commentaria* in c. 3, X, *de restitutione spoliatorum,* II, 13, n. 4.

[62] C. 2, *de poenis,* V, 8, in Clem.

[63] *Glos. Ord.* ad c. 2, *de poenis,* V, 8 in Clem., s.v. *omnino.*

[64] *Glos. Ord.* ad c. 2, *de poenis,* V, 8, in Clem., s.v. *modo supradicto.*

[65] *Commentaria* in c. 2, *de poenis,* V. 8, in Clem., nn. 7–8.

[66] C. 4, X, *de pactis,* I, 35; Jaffé, n. 13924.

[67] *Commentaria* in c. 4, X, *de pactis,* I, 35, n. 4.

[68] C. 8, X, *de pactis,* I, 35; Potthast, n. 9568.

Pope Paul II (1464–1471) declared in 1464 that any simoniacal dispositions made in reference to benefices, dignities or offices were invalid.[69] The general manner of speech on the part of the Pope in his decretal forces one to include resignation among the dispositions which the legislator nullified if they were infected with simony.

Article V. The Form of an Express Renunciation

There is no law in the *Corpus Iuris Canonici* which treats *ex professo* of the form to be observed in the execution of a resignation. Some information is available from Ioannes Andreae's commentary on a letter of Clement III (1187–1191). The Pope in this letter settled a case between two parties who were litigating about a benefice. One of the parties raised the exception of renunciation against the other party, and the Pope decided that witnesses should be introduced to solve the case.[70] From the fact that witnesses were to be brought in to prove the renunciation, Ioannes Andreae deduced that a renunciation could be made orally before witnesses as well as in writing.[71]

Likewise a decree of Clement V in the Council of Vienne (1311–1312) in settlement of a dispute about a resignation made by a proxy after his mandate had been recalled warrants the conclusion that a resignation could be made not only personally but also through the medium of a proxy.[72]

---

[69] C. 2, *de simonia,* V, 1, in Extravag. com.

[70] C. 5, X, *de renuntiatione,* I, 9; Jaffé, n. 16629.

[71] *Commentaria in Quinque Decretalium Libros* (Venetiis, 1581), in c. 5, X, *de renuntiatione,* I, 9.

[72] C. un., *de renuntiatione,* I, 4, in Clem.

CHAPTER III

THE DOCTRINE ON TACIT RENUNCIATION FROM THE DECREE OF GRATIAN TO THE COUNCIL OF TRENT

Subsequent to the treatment of express renunciation some discussion should also be devoted to a consideration of tacit renunciation. In a tacit renunciation no set form for the act of renunciation was called for. The office became vacant by the commission of certain acts with which the law associated the effect of a tacit renunciation on the part of the erstwhile incumbent.

In the period to be explored, it is rather difficult to determine precisely what acts or omissions constituted a tacit renunciation. The difficulty arises mostly from the legal terminology employed. Very often the terms "privation" and "renunciation" are used almost synonymously. In this chapter the writer has restricted himself to those cases which seem rather clearly to involve a tacit renunciation. Additional points could be raised concerning other cases of this period, but that would lead the discussion beyond its scope and purpose.

Article I. The Reception of Incompatible Offices

Incompatible offices were those which could not in law be possessed at one and the same time. The reason for the incompatibility could arise either from the nature of the offices themselves or from a positive prescription of the law. In the course of this article four cases of incompatibility will be treated, namely, the case of two offices to both of which the care of souls was attached, the case of two offices both of which required residence, the case of two prebends in the same church, and finally the case of the union of two benefices for one and the same incumbent when in itself one of the benefices sufficed for providing the requisite sustenance.

Alexander III was the first to issue a letter on this point in the Decretal law. He decreed that if anyone had two churches, it was necessary that he choose one of them and resign the other.[1] The same Pontiff issued another letter concerning a cleric who had the dignity of archdeacon in two churches. Once again the Pope ordered the person in question to choose one of them and to renounce the other.[2] The same Alexander III in a decree given in the III General Council of the Lateran (1179) declared that not more than one dignity was to be conferred upon any one person, and that a church was to be conferred upon one who was able to comply with the required residence and to exercise the required care in it. One lost his appointment to a church when he received it in a manner contrary to the prescriptions of the canons.[3] The Glossator noted that sometimes a person could serve his parish through a vicar when the church was annexed to a dignity or a prebend.[4]

Innocent III in the year 1205 included another case under the rule of incompatible offices when he forbade the holding of two prebends in the one church. He stated that the first prebend became vacant *ipso iure* and that its erstwhile incumbent had to renounce its possession.[5] The Glossator noted that the archbishop could grant a dispensation to hold both prebends in this case, but that the dispensation had to be given expressly. The mere confirmation of the second appointment was not sufficient to warrant the retention of both prebends.[6] He stated also that the bishop had the authority to dispense in the case of simple

---

[1] C. 7, X, *de praebendis et dignitatibus,* III, 5; Jaffé, n. 14168.

[2] C. 14, X, *de praebendis et dignitatibus,* III, 5; Jaffé, n. 13790.

[3] C. 3, X, *de clericis non residentibus in ecclesia vel praebenda,* III, 4; Mansi, XXII, 382.

[4] *Glos. Ord.* ad c. 3, X, *de clericis non residentibus in ecclesia vel praebenda,* III, 4, s.v. *per seipsum.*

[5] C. 9, X, *de concessione ecclesiae vel praebendae non vacantis,* III, 8; Potthast, n. 2505.

[6] *Glos. Ord.* ad c. 9, X, *de concessione ecclesiae vel praebendae non vacantis,* III, 8, s.v. *vacare noscatur.*

benefices or of a benefice with a church, but not in any cases in which the care of souls was involved.[7]

Innocent III in the IV General Council of the Lateran (1215) permitted a pastor to serve his parish through a vicar if the parish church had a dignity or a prebend attached to it.[8] The Glossator disagreed with those who concluded from this decree that a pastor could receive a prebend without the church becoming *ipso iure* vacant.[9] Hostiensis stated it as a lawful conclusion from this letter that a person could not have a prebend and a church at the same time if the church itself was sufficient as a benefice.[10]

Innocent III in the same general Council of the Lateran issued another decree in which he stated that if one possessed a benefice with the care of souls and received a second like benefice, the former became automatically vacant. Besides, if the person attempted to retain both benefices, then he lost the second one also.[11] The Glossator noted that this was a change from the law previously enacted in the decretal letters of Alexander III. Alexander III permitted the cleric to choose the benefice that he wished to retain, while Innocent III stated that the first benefice became automatically vacant by the reception of the second one.[12] Panormitanus attempted to reconcile these decretals by stating that the decretals of Alexander III had reference only to churches to neither of which was attached the care of souls, or to churches of which one did, but the other did not have the care of souls attached.[13]

Gregory IX in the year 1228 repeated the legislation of Innocent III by declaring in a decretal that if one had a dignity or a benefice with the care of souls and received another like

[7] *Glos. Ord. citing Ioannes Teutonicus,* ad c. 9, X, *de concessione ecclesiae vel praebendae non vacantis,* III, 8, s.v. *vacare noscatur.*

[8] C. 30, X, *de praebendis et dignitatibus,* III, 5; Mansi, XXII, 1016.

[9] *Glos. Ord.* ad c. 30, X, *de praebendis et dignitatibus,* III, 5, s.v. *praebendam.*

[10] *Commentaria* in c. 30, X, *de praebendis et dignitatibus,* III, 5, n. 16.

[11] C. 28, X, *de praebendis et dignitatibus,* III, 5; Mansi, XXII, 1015.

[12] *Glos. Ord.* ad c. 28, X, *de praebendis et dignitatibus,* III, 5, s.v. *contenderit.*

[13] *Commentaria* in c. 7, X, *de praebendis et dignitatibus,* III, 5, n. 7.

dignity or benefice, the former became vacant *ipso iure,* and if the party tried to retain both dignities or benefices, both of them became vacant.[14] The decretal also stated that a dispensation from the Holy See was required in order to permit one to hold two such benefices or dignities. Panormitanus contended that this was the best text to prove that the Holy See alone could dispense when there was incompatibility of offices by reason of the fact that the care of souls was attached to them. He stated also that there were two cases in which a cleric could hold two churches though both of them involved the care of souls, namely, when one was united to the other and when one was held in title and the other as a sinecure (*in commendam*).[15]

Gregory X (1271–1276) in the II General Council of Lyons (1274) commanded all ordinaries to inspect the dispensations of those who at that time were in possession of more than one benefice or dignity with the care of souls attached to them. In case of doubtful grants of dispensation recourse was to be made to the Holy See.[16] The Glossator called attention to the Holy See as the competent superior to grant a dispensation to hold more than one benefice or dignity involving the care of souls.[17]

Later, Boniface VIII, in speaking about the obtaining of a dispensation in such cases, insisted that in the request for the dispensation mention had to be made of every benefice that the person held at the time; otherwise the dispensation was null. A dispensation to hold two benefices involving the care of souls was to be understood as referring to the first two benefices which the persons received.[18] Boniface VIII likewise cautioned that, though the first benefice becomes vacant by the reception of a second one contrary to the rules regarding the incompatibility of benefices, and therefore the bishop could confer the first one immediately on some one else, nevertheless the person on whom it is conferred was not to take possession of it until it was sure

---

[14] C. 54, X, *de electione et electi potestate,* I, 6; Potthast, n. 8306.

[15] *Commentaria* in c. 54, X, *de electione et electi potestate,* I, 6, n. 9.

[16] C. 3, *de officio ordinarii,* I, 16, in VI°; Mansi, XXIV, 92.

[17] *Glos. Ord.* ad c. 3, *de officio ordinarii,* I, 16, in VI°, s.v. *sui beneficii.*

[18] C. 21, *de praebendis et dignitatibus,* III, 4, in VI°.

that the former incumbent had no right to retain it.[19] The Glossator remarked that perhaps the first incumbent had received a dispensation to hold both benefices, or was not receiving the fruits of the second one, or had the second one as a sinecure (*in commendam*). All these as reasons allowed him to retain the first one along with the second one.[20]

The same Boniface VIII made application of the law of incompatibility to priories or religious churches which had the care of souls attached to them. In this letter the Pope distinguished between those who at the time held two such churches or priories without the permission of the Pope, and those who were to receive them in the future. The former group had to choose between one or the other of the two churches within a month; the latter group could keep only the second church, since the first one would become vacant *ipso iure* when they received the second one.[21]

Clement V in the Council of Vienne (1311–1312) decreed that without a dispensation the reception of a dignity or of a benefice involving the care of souls produced the effect of a vacancy for all other like benefices or dignities which the person possessed.[22] The *Glossa Ordinaria* of Ioannes Andreae stated it as a natural consequence that, if the reception of a second benefice with the care of souls attached to it made the prior like benefice to be vacant, then it also made all other like benefices to be vacant for the same reason when more than one such benefice was held previously.[23]

In the same Council of Vienne Clement V decreed that, if a canonicate in a certain church had a prebend attached to it, then the one who possessed this prebend could accept the archdiaconate in the same church, even though this also had a prebend attached to it. But through the acceptance of the second prebend the first

---

[19] C. 28, *de praebendis et dignitatibus,* III, 4, in VI°.

[20] *Glos. Ord.* ad c. 28, *de praebendis et dignitatibus,* III, 4, in VI°, s.v. *retinendi.*

[21] C. 32, *de praebendis et dignitatibus,* III, 4, in VI°.

[22] C. 3, *de praebendis et dignitatibus,* III, 2, in Clem.

[23] *Glos. Ord.* ad c. 3, *de praebendis et dignitatibus,* III, 2, in Clem., s.v. *possessione.*

prebend was relinquished and thus became *ipso iure* vacant.[24] The Glossator remarked that it was evident from this decretal that the taking possession of a second prebend in the same church effected the vacancy of the former one.[25]

The final stage of development in the law on incompatibility of offices in this period appeared in a letter of Pope John XXII (1316–1334).[26] In this letter the Pope legislated for three distinct cases. Those who at the time of the letter were in possession of two or more dignities or benefices involving the care of souls and simultaneously enjoyed a dispensation to do so had to choose one with the care of souls and one without the care of souls if they wished to retain two benefices or dignities. This choice had to be made within a month, else all benefices were forfeited, and the person at fault became incapable of receiving any benefice with the attached care of souls in the future. Those who at the time of the letter held such benefices without the necessary dispensation could retain only the last one they had received and accordingly had to forfeit all the others. If they failed to observe this prescription, they forfeited all their benefices and became incapable of receiving in the future any type of benefice. Finally, those who in the future received a second benefice with the attached care of souls thereby occasioned the first one to become *ipso iure* vacant. Unless they relinquished the first benefice without delay, they lost both benefices and became incapable of receiving orders or any type of benefice in the future.

The *Glossa Ordinaria* of Zenzelinus de Cassanis (+1334) declared that the invoked penal sanction was of a *latae sententiae* character and no judicial sentence was required to deprive the offender of the first or the second benefice.[27] Regarding the law for the future as contained in this letter the Glossator seemed to think that the prohibition of receiving a second like dignity, personate, office or benefice was to be referred to all dignities,

---

[24] C. 6, *de praebendis et dignitatibus,* III, 2, in Clem.

[25] *Glos. Ord.* ad c. 6, *de praebendis et dignitatibus,* III, 2, in Clem., s.v. *hoc ipso.*

[26] C. un., *de praebendis et dignitatibus,* tit. III, in Extravag. Ioan. XXII.

[27] *Glos. Ord.* ad c. un., *de praebendis et dignitatibus,* tit. III, in Extravag. Ioan. XXII, s.v. *ipso iure secundo privati.*

offices or personates, even those which did not involve the care of souls, and to any office to which was attached the care of souls.[28]

As has been seen, the majority of texts was concerned with the incompatibility of offices which in connection with several benefices involved a multiple care of souls. The other categories of incompatibility were referred to in only one or two laws and glosses. The use of the terms, "prebend, office, dignity, personate," is at times quite confusing. It is difficult to decide whether these terms were used in an exclusive sense, or whether when mentioned singly they included the remaining three. In its final stage the law enacted that the taking of possession of a second incompatible office effected the vacancy of the former office. The fact that the law insisted that the incumbent of the office relinquish the former office or offices in the hands of the superior has to be understood as referring merely to the fact of possession and not to the title of the office. If he refused to comply with this rule, then he was automatically deprived of the second office as well. Throughout this period the Holy See was considered as the superior competent to grant dispensations for cases involving the care of souls in multiple benefices. The bishop appears to have been competent in other cases.

Article II. The Marriage of a Minor Cleric

The second way in which at least some clerics were considered tacitly to renounce their office was by their contracting of marriage. Here, too, the legislation is not unmistakably clear, but there are some definite conclusions that can be made.

In the Council of Neo-caesarea (314–325) it was stated that a priest who married was to be deposed from his order, and that a priest who committed fornication or adultery was to be put out of his church and reduced to penance among the laity.[29] The Glossator noted that the one who married lost his office but not his benefice, while the other type of offender lost everything. He was of the opinion that a priest who married was less an

---

[28] *Glos. Ord.* ad c. un., *de praebendis et dignitatibus,* tit. III, in Extravag. Ioan. XXII, s.v. *simile.*

[29] C. 9, D. XXVIII; Mansi, II, 545.

offender than the one who committed fornication or adultery, in view of the fact that the former believed that his action was permissible.[30]

Later the V Council of Carthage (401) decreed that if bishops, priests and deacons violated clerical continence, they were to be removed from their offices. Other clerics were permitted to follow the customs of their respective churches.[31]

Alexander II in a decree to the people of Milan between the years 1061 and 1073 stated that those who abandoned their divine office to commit fornication were deprived of their ecclesiastical office by such an act.[32] The same Pontiff in a letter to the bishops and the king of Dalmatia in the year 1062 declared that a bishop, priest or deacon who received a woman or retained one already received fell immediately from his position until satisfaction had been made.[33] The Glossator included subdeacons under this latter law.[34]

Later, Urban II (1088–1099) in the Council of Melfi in the year 1089 ruled that those who made use of marriage after receiving the subdiaconate were by that fact deprived of their office and benefice and were removed from the exercise of all sacred orders.[35]

Innocent II (1130–1143) in the Council of Rome (1139) declared that those who had received the subdiaconate and higher orders were deprived of their office and benefice if they married or kept concubines.[36] In an *Additio* Guido di Baysio (+1313), the Archdeacon of Bologna, expressed the opinion that a warning had to be given to the cleric before he was to be deprived of his office.[37] He was comparing the law of the Council of Rome with the later Decretal law. He stated that perhaps the Council of Rome did not require that a warning be given to the

---

[30] *Glos. Ord.* ad c. 9, D. XXVIII, s.v. *ordine.*

[31] C. 13, D. XXXII; Mansi, III, 969.

[32] C. 18, D. LXXXI.

[33] C. 16, D. LXXXI; Jaffé, n. 4477.

[34] *Glos. Ord.* ad c. 16, D. LXXXI, s.v. *diaconus.*

[35] C. 10, D. XXXII; Mansi, XX, 724.

[36] C. 2, D. XXVIII; Mansi, XXI, 526.

[37] *Additio of Guido di Baysio* (*Arch.*) ad c. 2, D. XXVIII.

cleric because of the fact that the Council was concerned with the case of a cleric who had actually married, while the later Decretal law was concerned with the case of a cleric who was guilty of keeping concubines, and therefore demanded that a warning be given to the cleric.

Alexander III, writing between the years 1159 and 1160, declared that a cleric in minor orders was deprived of his benefice if he married.[38] The same Pontiff in a letter to the Archbishop of Canterbury and his suffragans stated that clerics who did not abandon their concubines after having been warned were to be suspended from their benefice, and if they did not correct their manner of life, they were to be deposed.[39] The Glossator noted that this penalty was simply of the nature of a suspension, and that it did not take effect *ipso iure*.[40] In the same letter Alexander III decreed that clerics who had not yet received subdeaconship when they married had to give up their benefices, but were to retain their wives, while those who were in the order of subdiaconate or of higher orders when they married had to relinquish their wives and do penance.[41] The Glossator noted that those who were in minor orders were forced to give up their benefices when they married, for their benefices became vacant *ipso iure* by the placing of such an act. The constraint had reference only to the fact of possession, since married minor clerics tacitly renounced their right to the benefice by marrying. If married minor clerics were nevertheless allowed in given cases to keep their benefice, this permission must be considered as a specific favor which did not derive from the common law.[42] As regards those who were in major orders when they married, the Glossator remarked that they had to give up their wives, since the marriage was invalid. They were also to be deprived of their benefice for their infraction of the law through their attempt to contract

---

[38] C. 3, X, *de clericis coniugatis,* III, 3; Jaffé, n. 10608.

[39] C. 4, X, *de cohabitatione clericorum et mulierum,* III, 2; Jaffé, n. 13813.

[40] *Glos. Ord.* ad c. 4, X, *de cohabitatione clericorum et mulierum,* III, 2, s.v. *suspendatis.*

[41] C. 1, X, *de clericis coniugatis,* III, 3; Jaffé, n. 13813.

[42] *Glos. Ord.* ad c. 1, X, *de clericis coniugatis,* III, 3, s.v. *relinquenda.*

marriage.[43] Hostiensis was in agreement with the Glossator on the point that a minor cleric tacitly renounced his benefice by contracting marriage.[44]

Finally, Innocent III in a letter written in the year 1203 declared that the benefices in the possession of a cleric were to be taken from him when he married.[45] Hostiensis noted that the prescriptions of this letter applied only to clerics who were in minor orders when they married, since only minor clerics were considered to have tacitly renounced their benefice when they contracted marriage.[46]

It must be admitted that the legislation found on this point was not altogether clear. It is safe to say that those who were in minor orders tacitly renounced their benefices by marrying. The penalty for the marriage of a major cleric and for the keeping of concubines by any cleric seems to have been privation rather than simply a tacit renunciation of the benefice possessed by the delinquent cleric.

Article III. Solemn Religious Profession

There is a decretal letter of Boniface VIII, sent to the Chapter of the Church of Paris, which seems to indicate that solemn religious profession effected the tacit renunciation of a benefice.[47] In this letter the Pope stated that when one entered religion, his benefice was not to be conferred upon another person during the year of probation. He added, however, that it could be conferred on another if the person consented to it, or if it was evident that he was going to persevere in the religious life, or if he had made his religious profession, or had at least knowingly received the habit of the professed. The Glossator noted that this profession had to be one that was made in an approved religious institute.[48]

---

[43] *Glos. Ord.* ad c. 1, X, *de clericis coniugatis,* III, 3, s.v. *dimittere.*

[44] *Commentaria* in c. 1, X, *de clericis coniugatis,* III, 3, n. 2.

[45] C. 5, X, *de clericis coniugatis,* III, 3; Potthast, n. 1944.

[46] *Commentaria* in c. 5, X, *de clericis coniugatis,* III, 3, n. 1.

[47] C. 4, *de regularibus et transeuntibus ad religionem,* III, 14, in VI°.

[48] *Glos. Ord.* ad c. 4, *de regularibus et transeuntibus ad religionem,* III, 14, in VI°, s.v. *vel professionem.*

ARTICLE IV. VOLUNTARY MILITARY SERVICE

Pope Gregory IX in a letter written between the years 1227 and 1234 decreed that a cleric was to be deprived of his benefice if he failed to reëstablish residence when he had been warned to do so.[49] The Glossator noted that a cleric always had to be warned before he could be deprived of his benefice. He then invoked a distinction. If a cleric had evidently given up and abandoned his benefice (*habere pro derelicto*), then there was no need of a warning and the bishop could immediately confer the benefice upon another. Among the cases in which a cleric was considered to have completely given up and abandoned his benefice, the Glossator cited the one in which a cleric became a soldier. He put this act on a par with the act of contracting marriage and the act of receiving an incompatible office.[50] Since these latter acts were considered as tacit renunciations of one's benefice, the Glossator evidently considered the act of becoming a soldier also as a tacit renunciation of one's benefice.

---

[49] C. 17, X, *de clericis non residentibus in ecclesia vel praebenda,* III, 4; Potthast, n. 9628.

[50] *Glos. Ord.* ad c. 17, X, *de clericis non residentibus in ecclesia vel praebenda,* III, 4, s.v. *redierint.*

CHAPTER IV

THE DOCTRINE ON EXPRESS RENUNCIATION FROM THE COUNCIL OF TRENT TO THE CODE OF CANON LAW

ARTICLE I. THE SUBJECT AND OBJECT OF AN EXPRESS RENUNCIATION

Throughout the period after the Council of Trent (1545–1563) the general rule still held that any person could renounce an ecclesiastical office unless there was an express prohibition against it in the law. There existed, however, in this period a few more prohibitions by way of addition to those which were in force before the great Council.

SECTION 1. SUBJECTS WHO WERE EXCLUDED FROM RENOUNCING AN OFFICE

A—Major Clerics

The Council of Trent itself was responsible for the first new prohibition in this regard.[1] It forbade a major cleric to renounce the benefice to the title of which he had been ordained, unless he had another source of sufficient sustenance for the future. The violation of this prohibition entailed the invalidity of the resignation. The reason which the Council gave for enacting such a law was this: it sought to prevent a major cleric from falling under the necessity of begging or of procuring a livelihood from a source unbecoming to the dignity of his sacred orders.

Pope St. Pius V (1566–1572) later extended this prohibition to include the renunciation of any benefice possessed by a major cleric, whether the title of his ordination did or did not inhere in it.[2] The Congregation of the Council in 1726 decreed that

[1] Conc. Trident., sess. XXI, *de ref.*, c. 2.

[2] Const. "*Quanta Ecclesia,*" 1 apr. 1568—*Bullarum Diplomatum et Privilegiorum Romanorum Pontificum Tauriensis Editio* (25 vols., Augustae

proof had to be produced for the sufficient sustenance of a major cleric before he could be permitted to renounce his benefice. The oath of the cleric involved was not accepted as sufficiently conclusive to prove that fact.[3]

The Code of Canon Law today likewise forbids ordinaries to receive the renunciation of a benefice of a major cleric unless the cleric has another source of support. There is no invalidating clause in the law as it is stated in the Code.[4]

B—Novices

In order to insure absolute liberty to novices in the matter of making their religious profession, the Council of Trent nullified any renunciation made by a novice unless it was performed during the two months immediately preceding profession and with the permission of the bishop or his vicar.[5] The renunciation, even when made according to these rules, was not efficacious unless the profession actually followed. Since the Council spoke in a very general way of renunciation, a dispute arose as to whether the renunciation of a benefice came under this prohibition. Pirhing (1606–1679)[6] and Schmalzgrueber (1663–1735)[7] maintained that this prohibition included all types of renunciations, while Garcia (+ ca. 1613)[8] and Barbosa (1589–

Taurinorum, 1857–1872), VII, 664 (Hereafter this work will be cited as *Bullarium*); *Codicis Iuris Canonici Fontes cura Emi Petri Card. Gasparri editi* (9 vols., Romae: Typis Polyglottis Vaticanis, 1923–1939) (Vols. VII-IX ed. cura et studio Emi Iustiniani Card. Serédi), n. 125. Hereafter this work is cited as *Fontes.*

[3] S. C. C., *Lancianen.*, 9 febr. 1726, ad III et IV—*Thesaurus Resolutionum Sacrae Congregationis Concilii* (167 vols., Romae, 1718–1908) III, 275 (Hereafter this work is cited as *Thesaurus Resolutionum*); *Fontes*, n. 3311.

[4] *Codex Iuris Canonici Pii X Pontificis maximi iussu digestus, Benedicti Papae XV auctoritate promulgatus* (Romae: Typis Polyglottis Vaticanis, 1917. Reimpressio, 1933), canon 1484.

[5] Conc. Trident., sess. XXV, *de regularibus*, c. 16.

[6] *Jus Canonicum Nova Methodo Explicatum* (5 vols. in 4, Dilingae, 1674–1678), Lib. I, tit. IX, n. 25. Hereafter this work is cited as *Jus Canonicum.*

[7] *Jus Ecclesiasticum Universum* (5 vols. in 12, Romae, 1843–1845), lib. I, tit. IX, n. 15. Hereafter this work is cited as *Jus Ecclesiasticum.*

[8] *Tractatus de Beneficiis* (Coloniae Allobrogum, 1636), pars XI, c. I, n. 12.

1649)[9] limited its application to the renunciation of temporal goods. Pope Benedict XIV (1740–1758) decided this point in 1747 by stating that the prescriptions of the Council applied to the renunciation of both temporal goods and benefices.[10]

The Code of Canon Law also declares invalid the renunciation of a benefice made by a novice at any time during the period of the novitiate.[11]

C—Those Close to Death

In the *Regulae Cancellariae* of Clement XI (1700–1721) as collected by Reiffenstuel (1642–1703) there was the famous *Regula XIX,* according to which the renunciation made by a person within twenty days of his death was null.[12] This rule was effective even if the person was in good health at the time he made the renunciation.[13]

This law has been omitted from the present Code of Canon Law.

SECTION 2. A TYPE OF BENEFICE THAT COULD NOT BE RENOUNCED

The Council of Trent, besides requiring sufficient sustenance for a cleric who was resigning the benefice to the title of which he had been ordained, demanded also for the validity of the resignation that express mention be made of the fact that the benefice involved was the one to the title of which he had been ordained.[14]

The Code of Canon Law has retained this prohibition in canon 1485, where it declares that the renunciation of the benefice which served as the title of ordination to major orders is null unless the cleric expressly states that he was ordained on that title and has substituted another legitimate title with the permission of the ordinary.

---

[9] *De Officio et Potestate Episcopi* (3 vols. in 1, Lugduni, 1628), Alleg. XCIX, n. 19.

[10] Ep. "*Ex quo,*" 14 ian. 1747; *Fontes,* n. 374.

[11] Can. 568.

[12] *Jus Canonicum Universum* (5 vols. in 7, Parisiis, 1864–1882), lib. III, tit. V, par. XVI. Hereafter this work is cited as *Jus Canonicum.*

[13] Schmalzgrueber, *Jus Ecclesiasticum,* lib. I, tit. IX, n. 16.

[14] Conc. Trident., sess. XXI, *de ref.,* c. 2.

Article II. The Competent Superior for the Admission of an Express Renunciation

In the period which followed the Council of Trent there was little or no change in the legislation pertaining to the competent superior for the admission of renunciations of office. The Pope, the bishop and the legate *a latere* were still the more important superiors in this regard. It was still rather vague as to who was the competent superior with reference to those offices in regard to which different persons had the right of election or presentation and the right of institution. In all regards it seems that the rules of the earlier period continued in vogue.[15]

The necessity of the superior's consent for the renunciation of a benefice was declared to be an established point of law by a response of the Sacred Congregation of the Council.[16] Another response of the same Sacred Congregation declared that a resignation was not valid and perfect unless it was made before him who had the power of breaking the quasi-contract which was entered into between the incumbent and the church at the time the incumbent was appointed to the church by the superior.[17]

The Code of Canon Law states that for the validity of a resignation of office it is necessary that the renunciation be made to the person by whom it is to be accepted, or if it need not be accepted by anyone, that then it be made to the person from whom the office was received or to the one who holds his position. In cases wherein confirmation, institution or admission has place in the conferring of the office, the renunciation of the office must be made to the person who by law has the power of granting confirmation, admission or institution.[18]

---

[15] Cf. Reiffenstuel, *Jus Canonicum,* lib. I, tit. IX, n. 4; Pirhing, *Jus Canonicum,* lib. I, tit. IX, n. 29.

[16] S. C. C., *Nucerina,* 15 mart. 1828—Pallottini, *Collectio Omnium Conclusionum et Resolutionum quae in causis propositis apud Sacram Congregationem Cardinalium S. Concilii Tridentini Interpretum Prodierunt ab eius institutione, anno MDLXIV ad MDCCCLX distinctis titulis alphabetico ordine per materias digestas* (17 vols., Romae, 1868–1893), III, par. VII, n. 104. Hereafter cited as Pallottini.

[17] S. C. C., *Nullius seu Sublac. Institutionis,* 27 nov. 1852—Pallottini, III, par. VIII, n. 109.

[18] Can. 187.

Likewise according to the present Code a cleric who presumes to resign an office, benefice or dignity in the hands of the laity is by that very fact suspended *a divinis*.[19] This is a change from the previous law which stated that a cleric was to be deprived of his benefice for such an act.[20]

Article III. The Sufficient Cause Required for an Express Renunciation

In the period before the Council of Trent the question of a sufficient cause for the renunciation of an office was raised only in regard to the resignation of a bishop. The decretal of Pope Innocent III in 1206 provided the list of causes that were sufficient to permit the renunciation of an episcopal see.[21] This list had been considered an exhaustive list with reference to the resignations of bishops, but after the Council of Trent the authors disputed among themselves as to whether this list was meant to exclude the use of any other cause as a justification for a bishop's resignation. Pirhing,[22] Leurenius (1646–1723)[23] and Wernz[24] maintained that other good and useful causes proved sufficient to permit a bishop to renounce his see, while Schmalzgrueber[25] contended that the six causes listed by Innocent III were the only ones that were applicable with reference to the renunciation of a see by a bishop.

Pope St. Pius V was the first to introduce a list of causes which were considered sufficient for permitting the renunciation of a benefice inferior to the episcopal one. In his Constitution *Quanta Ecclesia,* he enumerated the sufficient causes with reference to these inferior benefices.[26] The constitution permitted bishops and other prelates to receive the resignations of those alone who could not or in law were not qualified to serve their benefice or church. The reason for such inability could be old age, sickness, crime

[19] Can. 2400.

[20] C. 8, X, *de renuntiatione,* I, 9; Potthast, n. 390.

[21] C. 10, X, *de renuntiatione,* I, IX; Potthast, n. 2698.

[22] *Jus Canonicum,* lib. I, tit. IX, n. 50.

[23] *Forum Beneficiale* (4 partes in 2, Venetiis, 1742), pars III, q. 406.

[24] *Ius Decretalium,* II, n. 496.

[25] *Jus Ecclesiasticum,* lib. I, tit. IX, n. 5.

[26] 1 apr. 1568—*Fontes,* n. 125.

or ecclesiastical censure. Likewise bishops could receive the resignations of those who contemplated the contracting of marriage or the entering of a religious institute, provided that these persons immediately fulfilled their intentions; besides they could receive the resignations of those who dared not or could not reside in the place of their benefice because of capital enemies. To these causes were added also the causes mentioned as applicable for bishops in the Decree of Innocent III.

A decision of the Sacred Roman Rota in 1796 declared that the prescriptions of the constitution of Pius V bound under pain of nullity and were applicable to the renunciation both of offices and of benefices.[27] Likewise a response of the Congregation of the Council stated it as an incontrovertible principle that the resignation of a benefice was invalid if it did not rest upon at least one of the causes listed by Innocent III and Pius V.[28]

The Code of Canon Law states merely that a just cause is required to permit a renunciation of an ecclesiastical office.[29] No mention is made of any specific types of causes, nor does the requirement of a just cause bind under pain of nullity. However, the Code does admonish superiors not to receive a renunciation of office without a just cause.[30]

Article IV. The Freedom Required in an Express Renunciation

Section 1. Freedom from Force and Fear

While in the period after the Council of Trent there was still an insistence on the necessity of excluding force and fear from renunciations of offices, nevertheless it remained uncertain as to whether the presence of these factors rendered a renunciation null or merely rescissible.

A decision of the Sacred Roman Rota in 1669 avoided the issue when it declared that a person should be reinstated in his benefice no matter whether the resignation was considered null

---

[27] *Sacrae Romanae Rotae Decisiones coram Consalvi* (Romae, 1822), dec. XLIII.

[28] S. C. C., *Rheginen.*, 18 maii 1850—*Thesaurus Resolutionum,* CIX, 193.

[29] Can. 184.

[30] Can. 189, § 1.

or merely rescissible. It stated that the authors of the time were divided in their opinion as to whether such a resignation was null or merely rescissible.[31]

Later a series of decisions was rendered by the Sacred Congregation of the Council in regard to the renunciation of a benefice if made under the influence of grave fear. The cleric claimed the presence of grave fear in the act of resignation and asked to be reinstated in the benefice. In the first of these decisions the Sacred Congregation decided for the nullity of the renunciation, but refused to permit the cleric to reclaim the benefice.[32] When the decision was appealed in the following year, the Sacred Congregation stood firm on its decision as to the nullity of the resignation, but decreed that the cleric could reclaim the benefice.[33] Another appeal was made in the case, and the Sacred Congregation, again holding for the nullity of the resignation, returned to the opinion that the cleric could not reclaim the benefice.[34] The following year the case was proposed once more for consideration. Then the Sacred Congregation, adding the definitive statement, *Et amplius,* answered that the resignation was null and that the cleric should be reinstated in the benefice if he was not given an equivalent benefice within six months.[35]

In another case before the same Sacred Congregation in the year 1880 a renunciation was declared to be valid. One of the alleged reasons for invalidity was the influence of grave fear in the resignation, but the Sacred Congregation considered the fear to be a just fear, since it arose from the fact that a trial was being instituted against the incumbent for the commission of a crime.[36]

These decisions seem to indicate that resignations made under the influence of grave fear, if unjustly inspired, were null. However, the authors of the time were not in accord on the

---

[31] *Sacrae Romanae Rotae Decisiones Recentiores* (ed. Farinacius, Rubeus, et Compagnus, 25 vols., Venetiis, 1697) pars XVI, dec. 212 (27 nov. 1669).

[32] S. C. C., *Baren.,* 17 maii 1851—*Fontes,* n. 4119.

[33] S. C. C., *Baren.,* 29 maii 1852—*Fontes,* n. 4121.

[34] S. C. C., *Baren.,* 18 sept. 1852—*Fontes,* n. 4129.

[35] S. C. C. *Baren.,* 28 maii 1853—*Fontes,* n. 4131.

[36] S. C. C., *Caietana,* 24 apr. 1880—*Fontes,* n. 4246.

point. Gonzalez-Tellez (+ after 1673) contended that force and fear invalidated a resignation *ipso iure*.[37] He based his decision on the decree of Clement V in the Council of Vienne, and on the fact that elections were null if force and fear entered into them. Schmalzgrueber, on the contrary, held that such resignations were valid but rescissible.[38] He retained the opinion of Panormitanus, who declared that the decree of Clement V applied only to resignations extorted by means of incarceration. He stated that although elections were nullified by force and fear, there was no law stating the same effect for resignations.

Pirhing did not attempt to solve the question at all; he merely stated that force, fear and deceit rendered a resignation either null or rescissible.[39] Barbosa,[40] Reiffenstuel,[41] Santi (1830–1885)[42] and Wernz[43] held that a renunciation motivated by force, fear or deceit was merely rescissible. Santi and Wernz noted, however, that absolute force and deceit which caused a substantial error caused a resignation to be *ipso iure* invalid.

The Code of Canon Law states clearly and unequivocally that grave unjust fear, deceit and substantial error render a renunciation of office *ipso iure* invalid.[44]

SECTION 2. FREEDOM FROM SIMONY

During the time of the Council of Trent and in the period following it there was a considerable amount of legislation on the subject of simony in reference to the resignation of offices and benefices. The policy of the earlier period, namely, of forbidding any type of pact in this regard, continued. The prescriptions, however, became even more specific.

[37] *Commentaria Perpetua in Singulos Textus Quinque Libros Decretalium Gregorii IX* (5 vols. in 4, Venetiis, 1699), lib. I, tit. XL, c. 4, n. 2.

[38] *Jus Ecclesiasticum,* lib. I, tit. IX, n. 4.

[39] *Jus Canonicum,* lib. I, tit. IX, n. 84.

[40] *Collectanea Doctorum tam Veterum quam Recentiorum in Jus Pontificium Universum* (6 vols. in 3, Lugduni, 1669), lib. I, tit. XL, n. 5.

[41] *Jus Canonicum,* lib. I, tit. XL, n. 30.

[42] *Praelectiones Iuris Canonici* (2 vols., Ratisbonae, Neo-Eboraci, Cincinnati, 1886), lib. I, tit. IX, n. 7. Hereafter this work is cited *Praelectiones.*

[43] *Ius Decretalium,* II, n. 497.

[44] Can. 185.

The Council of Trent in a general way excluded any reservation of access and of regress in regard to all types of benefices. For the acceptance of such reservations the Roman Pontiff alone was acknowledged as competent.[45] The intention of the Council was to avoid any species of hereditary succession in benefices. Likewise the Council forbade any reciprocal resignations of clerics in favor of their illegitimate sons, by which one might obtain the benefice of the other.[46]

During the time of the Council of Trent Paul IV (1555–1559) issued a *motu proprio* against the abuses current in the appointments to parishes and other benefices. He forbade the obtaining of a benefice for another with the hope of getting an annual pension or some other temporal benefit from him. Besides, he forbade the obtaining of benefices with the intention or pact of later resigning them in favor of another, even though no pension or other temporal benefit was involved in the transaction. The penalty attached to the violation of these prescriptions was an excommunication reserved to the Pope with the effect also that all the dispositions thus made were null and the benefice became reserved to the Holy See.[47]

Pius IV later declared that all pacts reserving pensions, or the right of ingress, regress or accession, were null and that the appointment to the benefice became reserved to the Holy See.[48]

Pius V in his Constitution *Quanta Ecclesia* warned the bishops and others who had authority in the conferring of benefices that they were not to allow the resigning party to indicate in any way who his successor should be. He also forbade these superiors to confer benefices and offices on the relatives and members of the household of the one who resigned them, or of the one who admitted the resignations.[49] The same Pontiff later approved the Constitution *Romanum Pontificem* of Pius IV, and set down

---

[45] Conc. Trident., sess. XXV, *de ref.*, c. 7.

[46] Conc. Trident., sess. XXV, *de ref.*, c. 15.

[47] Paulus IV, *motu. propr.*, "Inter caeteras," 27 nov. 1557—*Fontes,* n. 92.

[48] Pius IV, const. "*Romanum Pontificem,*" 17 oct. 1564—*Fontes,* n. 106.

[49] Pius V, "*Quanta Ecclesia,*" 1 apr. 1568—*Fontes,* n. 125.

rules and presumptions to be used in ascertaining when confidential simony was to be acknowledged as present in a case.[50]

Sixtus V (1585–1590) decided that if confidential simony had occurred in regard to a benefice, the bishop could make the appointment to the benefice provided that he had not participated in or consented to the crime.[51]

In 1703 the exchange of a benefice for a chaplaincy with the reservation of a pension from the benefice was not sustained by the Sacred Congregation of the Council.[52]

Benedict XIV in the year 1741 declared that pacts by which a cleric obtained a lump sum in place of the pension reserved to him by the Holy See at the time of his resignation were invalid. Likewise any payment of a lump sum in place of the pension within six months after the new incumbent took possession of the benefice was invalid, even though no proof was at hand that a past had intervened in this regard. Both offenders were deprived of the benefice and rendered incapable of obtaining any benefice in the future.[53]

In 1774 there was presented to the Sacred Congregation of the Council a case in which an untonsured person had received a chaplaincy and then resigned it on the condition that the patron should give it to a priest who would later return it to the young man when he had become a cleric. The cleric had already received the chaplaincy back from the priest, and the Sacred Congregation demanded that he resign the chaplaincy and restore the fruits he had received before he was entitled to ask for absolution from the censure attached to the crime of simony which he had committed.[54]

The same Sacred Congregation in 1789 stated that a resignation made in favor of a certain person, or with a reservation of prior rights, was simoniacal unless it was made in the hands

---

[50] Pius V, const. "*Intolerabilis,*" 1 iun. 1569—*Fontes,* n. 130.

[51] Sixtus V, "*Pastoralis officii,*" 13 aug. 1587—*Bullarium,* VIII, 895.

[52] S. C. C., *Novarien.,* 1 oct. 1703, ad I—*Fontes,* n. 3009.

[53] Benedictus XIV, const. "*In sublimi,*" 29 aug. 1741—*Fontes,* n. 317.

[54] S. C. C., *Caurien.,* 9 et 30 iul. 1774—*Fontes,* n. 3790.

of the Roman Pontiff.[55] Once again the same Sacred Congregation refused to approve a resignation of a benefice in which a pact was included, stating that it was confidential simony to enter such a pact without the permission of the Holy See according to the Constitution *Intolerabilis* of Pius V. It also stated that a contract of *do ut des* in regard to benefices was simoniacal.[56]

From all these pieces of legislation the authors before the Code of Canon Law drew their conclusions that a renunciation was simoniacal and null if any pact, condition or mode intervened by way of private agreement of the parties. In order that a resignation be made in favor of a third party, or with the reservation of a pension, or with the reservation of access, ingress or regress, it was necessary to have the permission of the Holy See.[57]

The Code of Canon Law declares a renunciation of office null if it is made simoniacally.[58] It also forbids the ordinary to confer on his own or the resigning party's household members, or the relatives by affinity or consanguinity up to and including the second degree, any office made vacant by an act of resignation. This prescription binds under pain of nullity.[59]

With reference to benefices the Code has retained the concept of confidential simony which prevailed before the Code. The Code forbids the ordinary to receive the renunciation of a benefice made for the benefit of another, or with any condition pertinent to the conferring of the benefice or to the sharing of the fruits, unless there be litigation about the benefice and one of the contending parties yield it in favor of the other litigant.[60] The Pontifical Commission for the Interpretation of the Code stated that the ordinary may accept the resignation of a pastor

---

[55] S. C. C., *Terracinen. seu Setina Cappellaniae,* 19 sept. 1789—*Thesaurus Resolutionum,* LVIIII, 208.

[56] S. C. C., *Nullius S. Iacobi de Spatha,* 21 apr. 1792—*Fontes,* n. 3878.

[57] Garcia, *Tractatus de Beneficiis,* pars XI, c. III, n. 145; Pirhing, *Jus Canonicum,* lib. I, tit. IX, n. 85; Reiffenstuel, *Jus Canonicum,* lib. I, tit. IX, n. 80; Santi, *Praelectiones,* lib. I, tit. IX, nn. 24–26; Wernz, *Ius Decretalium,* II, n. 498.

[58] Can. 185.

[59] Can. 157.

[60] Can. 1486.

with the reservation of a pension for the life of the pensioner, chargeable upon the parochial benefice in favor of the resigning pastor, but that the pension may not exceed one-third of the net revenue of the parish.[61]

Finally, the Code states that those who are guilty of simony with reference to ecclesiastical offices, benefices or dignities incur *ipso facto* an excommunication reserved in a simple manner to the Holy See, and are deprived perpetually of the right of election, presentation or nomination if they had such rights. Besides, clerics are to be suspended.[62]

ARTICLE V. THE FORM AND PUBLICATION OF AN EXPRESS RENUNCIATION

SECTION 1. THE FORM

As in the period before the Council of Trent, so in the post-Tridentine period it was possible to make a resignation through the medium of a proxy. This proxy could be a layman or a cleric, provided that he possessed a mandate empowering him to act.[63] Pirhing noted that in the Roman Curia the mandate had to be a public instrument, while private letters of deputation sufficed outside of that Curia.[64]

Schmalzgrueber [65] and Wernz [66] stated that, although the common law did not demand it, nevertheless the style of the Roman and Episcopal Curias required that the resignation be made in writing.

The Code of Canon Law requires for the validity of a renunciation of an ecclesiastical office that it be done by the resigning party either in writing or orally before two witnesses, or by a proxy having a special mandate.[67]

[61] 20 maii 1923, ad IX—*Acta Apostolicae Sedis, Commentarium Officiale* (Romae, 1909–), XVI (1923), 116. Hereafter cited as *AAS*.

[62] Can. 2392.

[63] Pirhing, *Jus Canonicum,* lib. I, tit. IX, n. 94; Schmalzgrueber, *Jus Ecclesiasticum,* lib. I, tit. IX, n. 41; De Angelis (1824–1881), *Praelectiones Iuris Canonici* (4 vols. in 6, Romae, 1877–1887), lib. I, tit. IX, n. 5 (Hereafter this work cited as *Praelectiones*).

[64] *Loc. cit.*

[65] *Op. cit.,* Lib. I, tit. IX, n. 39.

[66] *Ius Decretalium,* II, n. 497.

[67] Can. 186.

SECTION 2. THE PUBLICATION

The legislation after the Council of Trent added another element to the matter of a renunciation of a benefice, namely, the requirement that there be a publication made of the fact of resignation. This element was prescribed in detailed fashion by the Constitution *Humano vix iudicio* of Pope Gregory XIII (1572–1585) in 1584.[68] This Constitution demanded the publication of all renunciations of benefices tendered in the Roman Curia. This publication had to be made within six months from the time the resignation was tendered if the benefice was located on the Italian side of the Alps, and within nine months if it was on the farther side of these mountains. The publication was executed by the reading of the Apostolic letters in the church when the people were gathered for Solemn Mass. This had to be done in the church of the benefice and in the cathedral. If the church was a rural church and had no congregation, then the publication was to be made in the parish church in whose territory the benefice was located as well as in the cathedral. If war, pestilence or other danger interfered in these places, then the publication could be made in the nearest parish and cathedral churches.

The Constitution provided also for the publication of resignations which were tendered outside of the Roman Curia. It stated that the competent superior was to accept or reject the resignation within a month, and that the one promoted to the resigned benefice should publish the fact of his appointment and take possession of the benefice within three months.

All these requirements of the Constitution were stipulated as essential for the validity of the act and, if they were not observed, the conferral of the benefice became automatically reserved to the Holy See.

Benedict XIV in 1746 confirmed this constitution of Gregory XIII.[69]

The reason for this law was well explained by Pirhing.[70] He

---

[68] Gregorius XIII, const. "*Humano vix iudicio,*" 5 ian. 1584—*Fontes,* n. 152.

[69] Benedictus XIV, const. "*Ecclesiastica,*" 15 iun. 1746—*Continuatio Bullarii Romani Benedicti XIV* (3 vols. in 4, Prati, 1845–1847), II, 67.

[70] *Jus Canonicum,* lib. I, tit. IX, n. 103.

noted that it was introduced to avert all fraud and deception. In this way a person was prevented from later returning to take possession of the benefice under the pretext that he had not renounced it. Likewise parishioners were safeguarded from making mistakes as to who was their proper pastor. These and other deceptions were foiled and thwarted by the law of publication.

The Sacred Congregation of the Council declared in 1894 that the prescriptions of the Constitution *Humano vix iudicio* were essential requirements of validity, and that they were to be observed even though the act of renunciation was already well known.[71] Two years later the same Sacred Congregation stated that this form of publication was to be observed even if the *Regium Placet* should cause a delay in its execution.[72] The authors of the post-Tridentine period indicated, however, that the constitution of Gregory XIII had not been put into practice in all places.[73]

The Code of Canon Law makes no express mention of the publication of a resignation in the sense in which it was required before the Code. The Code requires that a written document of the resignation of an office be placed in the curial archives.[74] It also states that the renunciation must be accepted or rejected by the local ordinary within a month.[75] A response of the Commission for the Interpretation of the Code declared that a resignation may be accepted by the superior even after a month has elapsed, provided that the one who resigned has not withdrawn his renunciation and notified the ordinary of the withdrawal before the acceptance takes place.[76] Also the Code prescribes that notice of the accepted resignation should be sent as soon as possible to those who have any right in the matter of the conferring of the vacated office.[77]

---

[71] S. C. C., *Firmana,* 20 ian. 1894—*Analecta Ecclesiastica* (Romae, 1893-1911), II (1894), 69.

[72] S. C. C., *Apulana,* 25 iul. 1896—*Analecta Ecclesiastica,* IV (1896), 296.

[73] Garcia, *Tractatus de Beneficiis,* pars XI, c. I, n. 12; Reiffenstuel, *Jus Canonicum,* lib. I, tit. IX, n. 135; Santi, *Praelectiones,* lib. I, tit. IX, n. 29.

[74] Can. 186.

[75] Can. 189, § 2.

[76] 14 iul. 1922, ad. III—*AAS,* XIV (1922), 526-527.

[77] Can. 191, § 2.

CHAPTER V

THE DOCTRINE ON TACIT RENUNCIATION FROM THE COUNCIL OF TRENT TO THE CODE OF CANON LAW

The legislation on tacit renunciation did not undergo much change in the Council and in the period immediately following it. It is difficult at times to understand the nature of a tacit renunciation according to the explanations of the authors. Wernz, for example, seemed disinclined to admit the idea of a tacit renunciation. He preferred to speak of "*ablationes ob factum non-criminosum*" because of the fact that deprivations of office were enforced against a person even when he was unwilling to relinquish them.[1] In spite of differences on some points the general opinion of the authors was that a tacit renunciation was one by which a person was presumed by law to have the intention of resigning his office when he placed certain definite acts as enumerated in the law.[2]

The acts which were generally accepted as implying a tacit renunciation were identical with the acts thus characterized in the period before the Council of Trent, but with the present Code of Canon Law the law is extended to include acts heretofore not considered as implying a tacit renunciation at all.

Article I. The Reception of Incompatible Offices

The strong stand which the Church had already taken against the reception of a plurality of benefices was continued in the Council of Trent. The Council decreed in its seventh session that anyone attempting to hold several charges or otherwise incompatible benefices contrary to the sacred canons, and especially to the Constitution *De multa* of Innocent III, was *ipso*

[1] *Ius Decretalium,* II, n. 531.

[2] Schmalzgrueber, *Jus Ecclesiasticum,* lib. I, tit. IX, n. 2; Reiffenstuel, *Jus Canonicum,* lib. I, tit. IX, n. 9; Santi, *Praelectiones,* lib. I, tit. IX, n. 3.

facto deprived of these benefices.[3] In the same session it was forbidden to hold at the same time several metropolitan or cathedral churches. Those who were holding them at the time could choose the one they preferred, but had to resign all the others within six months if the churches were subject to the free conferral of the Holy See, or within a year in other cases. If they failed to do this, then all the churches except the one latest received were considered *ipso facto* vacant.[4] Likewise local ordinaries were commanded to examine the dispensations of those who at the time were holding several charges or otherwise incompatible benefices.[5]

The same Council ordered also that only one ecclesiastical benefice could be conferred upon a person. If that was not sufficient for the sustenance of the cleric, then the ordinary could confer also a simple benefice on him, provided that not both of them required the personal residence of the cleric. This regulation applied in relation to all benefices. If anyone at the time of the Council possessed more than one parochial church, or one cathedral and one parochial church, he had to choose the one he wished to retain and resign the others within six months. Otherwise all became vacant and could then be conferred upon others.[6]

Some responses of the Sacred Congregation of the Council help to clarify the meaning and the extension of the decrees of the Council of Trent. One response given on August 14, 1632, stated that the taking of possession of the second incompatible benefice effected the vacancy of the first one, and the second one also became vacant if the cleric attempted to retain possession of both benefices.[7] Another response of the same date decided that the chancery rule of triennial possession could not be used by one possessing a plurality of incompatible benefices. Both incompatible benefices became vacant when a person who was already in possession of one sufficient benefice received another one and

[3] Conc. Trident., sess. VII, *de. ref.*, c. 4.

[4] *Ibid.*, c. 2.

[5] *Ibid.*, c. 5.

[6] Conc. Trident., sess. XXIV. *de ref.*, c. 17.

[7] S. C. C., *Hispalen,* 14 aug. 1632—*Fontes,* n. 2546.

retained the fruits of both benefices, even though this practice had continued for a period of two years.[8] Still another response of the same date cleared up an additional point when it stated that a bishop was permitted to confer but one additional simple benefice on a cleric who possessed a simple benefice which was insufficient to provide him with a livelihood.[9]

In the same vein a later response of the Sacred Congregation declared that an Apostolic dispensation was necessary to enable a cleric to retain three simple benefices received from lay patrons, even though the benefices were not in the same church.[10]

With the advent of the Council of Trent, then, the distinction between two types of incompatible benefices, namely, those with reference to which a vacancy was effected *ipso iure* and those which required a sentence of privation to effect the vacancy, was abandoned. As Reiffenstuel noted,[11] the Council of Trent stated that the reception of a second benefice which was in any way incompatible with the first one effected the vacancy of the first one *ipso iure*. Fagnanus (1598–1678) remarked that the Council of Trent extended the penalty of the Decretal, *De multa*, of Innocent III to all incompatible benefices. The option, given by Alexander III, of choosing one or the other of the incompatible benefices applied after the Council of Trent only to the case of two incompatible benefices which were acquired at the same moment of time. In such a case, since both benefices were received at the same moment, one could not be accused of receiving a second benefice while already in possession of a prior incompatible one.[12] Santi specified personal residence and sufficient sustenance as the elements from which incompatibility of benefices arose.[13] De Angelis maintained that the only two compatible benefices were those of which the first one received

---

[8] S. C. C., *Leodien.*, 14 aug. 1632—*Fontes*, n. 2547.

[9] S. C. C., *Aquilana*, 14 aug. 1632—*Fontes*, n. 2545.

[10] S. C. C., *Cursolen.*, 13 maii 1651—Santi, *Praelectiones*, lib. III, tit. V, n. 79.

[11] *Jus Canonicum*, lib. III, tit. V, n. 293.

[12] *Commentaria in V Libros Decretalium* (4 vols., Venetiis, 1697), lib. III, tit. V, c. VII, n. 9–10.

[13] *Praelectiones*, lib. III, tit. V, n. 79.

was not adequate for providing the incumbent with a fit sustenance.[14]

The Code of Canon Law states that a cleric loses his first office through a tacit renunciation when he receives and takes possession of a second incompatible office.[15] According to the Code offices are incompatible when their inherent duties can not be fulfilled by the same person at one and the same time.[16] Benefices are incompatible for the same reason, but furthermore also if one of them is sufficient for the sustenance of the incumbent.[17] If a person receives a second incompatible benefice or office, and then tries to retain the prior one also, the law deprives him automatically of both.[18]

Article II. The Marriage of a Cleric

The marriage of a minor cleric continued after the Council of Trent to be a factor which entailed the tacit renunciation of an office. The question most considered in this period was whether an invalid marriage had the same effect as a valid marriage in this matter. On this point there existed a variety of opinions.

Riganti (1661–1735) contended that a null marriage had the same effect as a valid marriage in this regard, except when the nullity was caused by a lack of consent, as, for example, in the case of a child or of an insane person.[19] He referred to a response of the Sacred Congregation of the Council which declared that a certain Caius could not resign his benefice, since it had already become vacant by his contracting of marriage, even though the marriage was performed without the witnesses required for its validity by the law of the Council of Trent. It was immaterial whether or not the person involved knew of the

---

[14] *Praelectiones,* lib. III, tit. V, n. 23.

[15] Can. 188, n. 3.

[16] Can. 156, § 2.

[17] Can. 1439, § 2.

[18] Can. 2396.

[19] *Commentaria in regulas, constitutiones, et ordinationes cancellariae apostolicae* (4 vols. in 2, Coloniae Allobrogum, 1751), in reg. LVIII, sec. III, nn. 21, 30.

nullity of the marriage. Leurenius was of the same opinion as Riganti.[20]

Others made distinctions between the different types of nullity. Garcia [21] and Barbosa [22] claimed that the benefice did not become vacant if the marriage was null because of the lack of consent or the non-observance of the prescribed Tridentine form of marriage, but that it did become vacant if the cleric contracted a marriage, even when he was conscious of the fact that a diriment impediment stood in the way of the validity of this union. Sanchez (1550–1610),[23] Santi [24] and De Angelis prescinded entirely from the intention of the cleric and claimed that a benefice was not tacitly renounced as long as the marriage was null for any reason whatsoever. They claimed that the reason for the law was based on the incompatibility of the marital and the clerical states, and as long as the marriage was null, there could be no question of incompatibility. Wernz agreed with Riganti, holding that any marriage, valid or invalid, effected the vacancy of a benefice as long as the nullity of the marriage did not arise from a lack of consent.[25]

Those who claimed that the intention of the party, and not the validity of the marriage, was the predominant thing to be considered took their opinion from a case in the Decretals.[26] In this case a man who had received major orders after his wife had died later married another woman. He was subjected to the penalties of a bigamist in spite of the fact that the second marriage was null by reason of his sacred orders. From this fact these authors argued that the intention of the cleric was the important element to be considered. Hence some authors held that if a cleric contracted marriage in ignorance of the presence of a diriment impediment, his marriage, though invalid, would

---

[20] *Forum Beneficiale,* pars III, q. XLIV–XLVI.

[21] *Tractatus de Beneficiis,* pars. XI, c. VIII, nn. 1–15.

[22] *De Officio et Potestate Episcopi,* Alleg. LVII, n. 207.

[23] *De Sancto Matrimonii Sacramento Disputationum Libri Dacem in Tres Tomos Distributi* (Venetiis, 1712), lib. VII, disp. XIII, n. 4.

[24] *Praelectiones,* lib. III, tit. III, nn. 5–7.

[25] *Ius Decretalium,* II, n. 532.

[26] C. 4, X, *de bigamis,* I, 21; Potthast, n. 700.

effect a tacit renunciation; on the other hand, if he knew of the presence of the diriment impediment, he could not be accused of a tacit renunciation. Many other distinctions were made by the authors, but the ones already indicated were the important ones.

A response of the Sacred Congregation of the Council stated that a benefice became vacant in consequence of marriage except when consent was lacking in the marriage, for in such a case the will of taking a wife and of abandoning the clerical state was not present.[27] Likewise a conclusion drawn from another response of the same Sacred Congregation stated without any limitation that the marriage of a minor cleric caused his tacit renunciation of the benefice.[28] An article in Volume XI of the *Acta Sanctae Sedis* still held the opinion that a minor cleric did not renounce his benefice in the event of marriage which was null because of the non-observance of the prescribed Tridentine form of marriage.[29]

The Code of Canon Law states that a cleric, major or minor, tacitly renounces an ecclesiastical office by contracting even a so-called civil marriage.[30]

Article III. Religious Profession

In the period after the Council of Trent solemn religious profession in a religious order continued to be a factor that entailed the tacit renunciation of a benefice. For those who made simple profession a benefice did not become vacant by profession, but they could be forced to resign it if the benefice was a residential one. If they did not resign it, then the bishop could proceed against them.[31]

In the year 1903 the Sacred Congregation for Bishops and Regulars decided that in the Congregation of the Missionaries

---

[27] S. C. C., *Brixinen.*, 18 sept. 1790—*Thesaurus Resolutionum,* LVIII, 191.

[28] S. C. C., *Reintegrationis seu Rehabilitationis in Paroeciam,* 28 iul. 1877—*Acta Sanctae Sedis* (41 vols., 1865-1908), XI (1878), 38. Hereafter cited as *ASS.*

[29] *ASS,* XI (1878), 43.

[30] Can. 188, n. 5.

[31] S. C. C., *Pinerolien.,* 23 nov., 14 dec. 1833—*Thesaurus Resolutionum,* XCIII, 432, 449.

of the Immaculate Heart of Mary perpetual profession effected the vacancy of residential benefices, and thus the members did not need to have recourse to the Sacred Congregation in order to renounce their benefice before their profession.[32] Wernz remarked that it was not clear whether other types of benefices were affected by such a profession, or whether the response of the Sacred Congregation was applicable to all congregations in which a perpetual profession was made.[33]

The Code of Canon Law states that any type of religious profession causes the tacit renunciation of an ecclesiastical office.[34] In the matter of benefices there are some restrictions in this regard. Parochial benefices become vacant only one year after the profession, while other benefices become vacant only three years after the profession.[35]

Article IV. Voluntary Military Service

The legal disposition of this point continued to hinge on the remark of the Glossator for whatever legal force it had. No legislation was added on the point, but there were a few decisions of the Sacred Congregation of the Council which seemed to confirm the opinion which had been traditional in its acceptance by the authors.

The first response in 1788 contained a statement that a cleric who volunteered for military service lost all benefices, since he was considered to have chosen a state of life incompatible with the clerical one. Even if he abandoned the military life later, he was not to be reinstated in the benefice.[36] The same opinion was stated two years later in another case before the same Sacred Congregation.[37]

The Code of Canon Law forbids a cleric to volunteer for military service unless he do it with the ordinary's permission

---

[32] S. C. Ep. et Reg., 25 aug. 1903—*Fontes,* n. 2045.

[33] *Ius Decretalium,* II, p. 270, footnote 5.

[34] Can. 188, n. 1.

[35] Can. 584.

[36] S. C. C., *Firmana Cappellaniae,* 7 iun. 1788—*Thesaurus Resolutionum,* LVI, 93.

[37] S. C. C., *Brixinen.,* 18 sept. 1790—*Fontes,* n. 3871.

for the purpose of being more quickly freed of the obligation.[38] A cleric who violates this rule loses his office by a tacit renunciation.[39]

[38] Can. 141, § 1.
[39] Can. 188, n. 6.

PART TWO

CANONICAL COMMENTARY

Although an express renunciation and a tacit renunciation of an ecclesiastical office produce the same effect in the law, namely, the vacancy of the ecclesiastical office, they differ greatly in regard to the manner in which they are executed. An express renunciation must be made in accordance with a variety of rules and formalities; a tacit renunciation, on the other hand, requires nothing more than the placing or the omission of the act to which the law has attached the effect of a tacit renunciation. Because of this essential difference between these two types of renunciation, it is necessary to discuss them separately.

The writer calls to mind once more the fact that only an ecclesiastical office in the strict sense is under consideration in this work.

CHAPTER VI

THE LEGITIMATE SUBJECT AND OBJECT OF AN EXPRESS RENUNCIATION

> Canon 184. *Quisque sui compos potest officio ecclesiastico iusta de causa renuntiare, nisi speciali prohibitione renuntiatio sit ipsi interdicta.*

With this canon the Code formulates the general rule with reference to the subject and object of an express renunciation. The general tenor of the canon gives the impression that the Church does not wish to render unduly difficult the renunciation of an ecclesiastical office. Although the canon itself makes provision for exceptions to the general rule, there are in reality few exceptions. Provided that a cleric has the use of reason and can present a just cause for renouncing his office, it is rare that the resignation may not be made by the incumbent and accepted by the superior. The Church is always reasonable in her demands, and while she feels free to impose obligations on her subjects, she is ever ready to release them from these obligations when the proper circumstances warrant such a release. An analysis of the elements in canon 184 will demonstrate the truth of this principle. Through this analysis it will become clear as to who may renounce an ecclesiastical office and what ecclesiastical offices may be renounced. It is necessary to settle these two fundamental points before proceeding to the treatment of the rules for the actual execution of an express renunciation of an ecclesiastical office.

Article I. The Mental Capacity of the Subject

The Code, in demanding that a cleric have the use of his reason in order to renounce an office, merely restates a principle of the natural law. The renunciation of an office must be a human act, and to be such the person must have the use of his faculties at the time of the renunciation. Otherwise the resignation is by the natural law invalid.

The loss of the use of reason may be a habitual state as in the case of an idiot, or it may be only temporary, arising, for example, from drunkenness, fear, sleep, vehement passion or any other like source. The source or the nature of the deficiency does not receive any consideration.[1] Even if a person has lost the use of his reason through some fault of his own, as, for example, in the case of voluntary drunkenness, a resignation made while he is in such a condition is invalid. The law makes no distinction since the use of reason is a prerequisite for any human act. At most the law could punish an individual for permitting himself to be deprived of the use of his faculties through his own fault, but there could be no possibility of taking the resignation under serious consideration. In brief, the mental capacity of the incumbent must be such as to permit him to know what he is doing at the time of his resignation. If this condition is not

[1] Coronata, *Institutiones*, I, n. 262.

verified, then the person is incapable of validly renouncing an ecclesiastical office.

Article II. The Requirement of a Just Cause

Although the Church permits a reasonable amount of freedom in the renunciation of an ecclesiastical office, she could not be expected to permit such resignations without a just cause. If an arbitrary freedom were granted in this matter, it would inevitably result in grave detriment to the Church and to souls.[2]

The Code makes mention of the requirement of a just cause in two instances. The present canon requires a just cause to permit the incumbent to renounce his office, while a later canon [3] forbids the superior to accept a resignation without a just and proportionate cause. These canons are not to be interpreted in the sense that two distinct just causes are necessary, one to justify the incumbent's resignation and another to justify the superior's acceptance of the resignation. The same cause may and ordinarily will be used to justify both of these acts.[4] One could perhaps expect that the requirement of a just cause should receive mention only with reference to the acceptance of the resignation by the superior, since it is he who must ultimately judge concerning the existence of the proportionate cause in each resignation. However, since the Code does not require that every resignation be accepted by the superior,[5] it was necessary to mention the requirement of a just cause also in connection with the active subject of a resignation.

Since the Code does not supply any list of specific causes, it is necessary for the superior to judge concerning the cause in each individual case. Ecclesiastical offices vary in dignity and importance, and for this reason it is necessary that the just cause vary in the same proportion, for the law requires that the cause be a proportionate one. The more important the office is, the more grave the cause must be to permit the resignation of that office. The office of bishop, for example, demands a more serious

[2] Wernz-Vidal, *Ius Canonicum,* II, n. 327.

[3] Can. 189, § 1.

[4] Coronata, *Institutiones,* I, n. 263.

[5] E. g., the resignation of a vicar capitular—Can. 443.

cause to justify its resignation than does the office of pastor, since the former office is of much greater importance. A more grave cause may be required for the renunciation of a specific office because of the circumstances, as, for example, when the present incumbent is the only person capable of fulfilling the duties of the office under consideration. The just cause, then, at times must be necessarily a grave cause in order that it be in proportion to the office which is to be renounced.

The legislation of the pre-Code period provided some specific causes which may serve as an aid to the superior in determining the presence of a just cause in an individual case. Innocent III drew up a list of causes which were recognized as sufficient to permit a bishop to ask permission to renounce his see.[6] Pius V in like manner formulated a list of causes which were accepted as sufficient to warrant the renunciation of an office inferior in dignity to the episcopal office.[7] The two lists were substantially the same, although the latter list did contain a greater variety of causes, since it had reference to inferior offices. The authors were occustomed to summarize the sufficient causes by means of the following verse:

Debilis, ignarus, male conscius, irregularis,
Quem mala plebs odit, dans scandala cedere possit.

Although these causes are not specifically mentioned in the present law, according to which any just and proportionate cause permits one to renounce his office, nevertheless they can be useful for the determination of the present just and proportionate cause. Cocchi notes that the cause may have reference to the good of the Church, to the good of souls or to the good of the incumbent himself.[8] It is worthy of note also that the cause may have reference to a temporal good as well as to a spiritual one.

In spite of the fact that the requirement of a just cause must be considered of great importance, it must be admitted that it is not necessary for the validity of a resignation in the present law. Canon 184 is not so worded as to incorporate the elements which

---

[6] C. 10, X, *de renuntiatione,* I, 9; Potthast, n. 2698.
[7] Const., "*Quanta Ecclesia,*" 1 apr. 1568—*Fontes,* n. 125.
[8] *Commentarium,* II, n. 98.

are necessary in order that a law may be considered as an invalidating law.[9]

Article III. Special Prohibitions in Regard to the Subject and Object

Although canon 184 states that anyone mentally capable may renounce an ecclesiastical office provided that he have a just cause for so doing, it does not set this down as an inviolable rule. The canon itself leaves room for exceptions to this rule by the addition of a *nisi* clause which recognizes the possibility of special prohibitions against the renunciation of an office. These special prohibitions may arise from either the common law or the particular law. Maroto states that particular law in some religious institutes forbids the renunciation of an office which has been received by a religious from the chapter or from a major superior.[10] In this discussion only the prohibitions which are enacted in the Code will be considered. This will be followed by a discussion on the power of the ordinary to establish prohibitions against the renunciation of offices in the diocese.

Section 1. Novices

In order to insure the greatest possible freedom to a novice in the making of his religious profession in a religious institute, the Code renders null and void the renunciation of a benefice made by a novice during the period of the novitiate.[11] This prohibition applies to the renunciation of a benefice by a novice in any religious institute, even though the institute is merely of diocesan right.[12] Schäfer notes that this prohibition does not affect a resignation which is made prior to one's entry into the novitiate.[13]

---

[9] Can. 11.—*Irritantes aut inhabilitantes eae tantum leges habendae sunt, quibus aut actum esse nullum aut inhabilem esse personam expresse vel aequivalenter statuitur.*

[10] *Institutiones,* I, n. 679.

[11] Can. 568, § 1.

[12] Vermeersch-Creusen, *Epitome,* I, n. 715.

[13] *Compendium de Religiosis ad Normam Codicis Juris Canonici* (2. ed., Münster i. W.: Ex Officina Libraria Aschendorf, 1931), n. 251. Hereafter cited as *De Religiosis.*

The wisdom of this prohibition is quite obvious. If a person were permitted to renounce his benefice during the time of the novitiate, his anxiety about his future sustenance might be so great as to prompt him to make his religious profession when in reality he preferred to return to the world.

SECTION 2. MAJOR CLERICS

A canonical title is required by the law for the licit ordination of a cleric to major orders.[14] The canonical title is a provision for a decent and perpetual sustenance of a cleric who receives major orders.[15] The Code provides a variety of canonical titles, but only one is of interest here, namely, the title of benefice, which is enumerated first among the legitimate canonical titles for secular clerics.[16]

In order to prevent a cleric in major orders from falling under the necessity of begging or of procuring a livelihood from a source unbecoming to the dignity of his sacred orders, the Code enacts a special prohibition with reference to the renunciation of the benefice to the title of which the major cleric was ordained. The law renders invalid such a resignation unless express mention is made in the resignation of the fact that the cleric was ordained to that title and that another legitimate title has been substituted for it with the consent of the ordinary.[17] Hence for the validity of such a resignation three things are necessary, namely, an express mention of the peculiar quality of the benefice, the substitution of another legitimate title, and the consent of the ordinary to such a substitution. The legitimate title which is subsituted may be any one of those which are recognized as canonical titles of ordination in canons 979, § 1, and 981, § 1.[18]

The care of the Church in guaranteeing a decent sustenance to her clerics in major orders is manifested still further by the

---

[14] Can. 974, n. 7.

[15] Vermeersch-Creusen, *Epitome,* II, n. 250.

[16] Can. 979, § 1.

[17] Can. 1485.

[18] Augustine, *A Commentary on the New Code of Canon Law* (8 vols., Vol. II, 6. ed., 1936; Vol. VI, 3. ed., 1931; Vol. VIII, 3. ed., 1931, St. Louis: Herder Book Co.), VI, 543. Hereafter this work is cited as *A Commentary.*

prescriptions of canon 1484. This canon forbids the ordinary to receive the resignation of a major cleric with reference to any type of benefice unless it is certain that the cleric has another source from which to derive a decent support. This certitude concerning the source of his future support may be derived from documents, witnesses or from any other reliable source of information.[19]

Canon 1484 safeguards the prescriptions of canon 584 which states that parochial benefices become vacant one year after a religious profession has been made, and other benefices become vacant three years after such a profession. In these circumstances there is a tacit renunciation, but it does not take effect until the prescribed time has elapsed.[20] The prohibition in canon 1484, unlike the prohibition in canon 1485, does not affect the validity of the resignation.

SECTION 3. CONDITIONAL RENUNCIATION OF BENEFICES

Canon 1486 forbids the ordinary to receive the renunciation of a benefice in favor of another person or with an attached condition which affects the conferral of the benefice or the distribution of the fruits of the benefice, unless there be litigation about the benefice, and one of the contending parties yields the benefice to the other litigant.

The prohibition of resigning in favor of another person is made to avert the danger of simony or any species of hereditary succession in benefices.[21] Canon 1486 makes one exception to this prohibition. If there is litigation about the benefice, the ordinary may admit the resignation of the benefice when it is made by one of the contesting parties in favor of the other litigant. Vermeersch-Creusen state that this exception is made in the interest of peace.[22]

In order that such a resignation may be permitted, the benefice must be truly under litigation. This means that the summons

[19] Blat, *Commentarium,* III, Pars altera, n. 392.

[20] Can. 188, n. 1.

[21] Conc. Trident., sess. XXV, *de ref.,* c. 7; Pius V, const. *"Quanta Ecclesia,"* 1 apr. 1568—*Fontes,* n. 125.

[22] *Epitome,* II, n. 809.

must have been duly issued and legitimately served or that the parties have spontaneously appeared in court.[23] Likewise, in order to permit such a resignation, the benefice must be one which the ordinary has the power freely to confer. Otherwise the promoter of justice must continue the case in the interest of the freedom of the benefice, even after the other litigant has renounced his claim to it.[24]

Besides forbidding the ordinary to receive the renunciation of a benefice in favor of another, canon 1486 also forbids the admission of a resignation with an attached condition which affects the conferral of the benefice or the distribution of its fruits.

The subsequent conferral of the benefice may be affected in various ways by the attaching of conditions from the side of the resigning incumbent. It may be a condition which limits the conferral of the benefice in such a way that it can be conferred only upon a cleric of a certain town or of a certain nationality. On the other hand, it may be a condition which reserves the right of the resigning party to return to the possession of the benefice at a later date. If any such conditions are attached to the resignation of a benefice, the ordinary is forbidden to admit such a resignation. By such conditions the freedom of appointment to the benefice is greatly hampered.

Finally, canon 1486 forbids the ordinary to accept a resignation with a condition affecting the distribution of the fruits of the benefice. This prohibition is in conformity with the law which states that benefices are to be conferred without diminution.[25] It is permissible, however, for the ordinary to establish a pension and to impose its payment upon the benefice for the lifetime of the officeholder. Such an imposition of a pension must be made at the time the benefice is conferred, and express mention of the pension must be made in the act of conferral. Likewise a fit portion of the fruits must be guaranteed to the incumbent. In the case of a parochial benefice the pension may be imposed only in favor of the retiring pastor or vicar of that benefice, and the pension may not exceed one-third of the net

[23] Pistocchi, *De re beneficiali* (Taurini: Marietti, 1928), p. 487.

[24] Can. 1734; cf. Blat, *Commentarium,* III, Pars altera, n. 394.

[25] Can. 1440.

revenue of the benefice.[26] The Pontifical Commission for the Interpretation of the Code has given a response to the effect that an ordinary may accept the resignation of a pastor with the reservation of a pension chargeable to the benefice for the lifetime of the pensioner provided that the pension does not exceed one-third of the net revenue of the benefice.[27]

The Sacred Congregation of the Council had previously stated that when a pastor is asked to resign in accordance with canon 2148, § 1, with the provision that he will receive a life-long pension not exceeding one-third of the net revenue of the parish, such a resignation is not to be considered a conditional one. In such a case the resignation is asked for and given absolutely. The pension involved is merely the ordinary's method of providing for the resigning pastor by means of a pension in accordance with canon 2154, § 1, which contemplates such provision.[28]

Since the Code restricts the right of the ordinary to receive conditional resignations, they may be accepted only on the authority of the Roman Pontiff. Such resignations made without the Pope's authority constitute confidential simony and they will be discussed from that point of view in the section of this work set aside for a treatment of simony in the renunciation of an ecclesiastical office.

In the opinion of the writer the prohibitions as mentioned in the present article are the only ones enacted in the common law. As has been seen, they all refer only to offices which are at the same time benefices, and for this reason the discussion of each prohibition has been brief, since this work is dedicated primarily to the renunciation of an ecclesiastical office in general.

Some authors mention that a cleric is forbidden to renounce his ecclesiastical office if because of the commission of a crime he has been deprived of it either *ipso iure* or by means of a condemnatory sentence of the judge,[29] but the writer does not consider this as a prohibition. The cleric in either case has

---

26 Can. 1429, §§ 1–2.

27 20 maii 1923, ad IX—*AAS,* XVI (1924), 116.

28 11 nov. 1922—*AAS,* XV (1923), 454.

29 Wernz-Vidal, *Ius Canonicum,* II, n. 325; Cocchi, *Commentarium,* II, n. 98.

already lost all right to the office. Other authors maintain that a cleric who is still a minor is forbidden to renounce his ecclesiastical office without the permission of his parents or guardians.[30] They argue from canon 89, which states that minors in the exercise of their rights are subject to their parents or guardians except in those things in which the law exempts them from such dependence. Since they fail to see any exemption in the Code with reference to the renunciation of an office, they maintain that a minor depends upon his parents or guardians in the execution of such an act.

The writer believes that the Code does exempt minors from this dependence at least implicitly with reference to the renunciation of an cclesiastical office. The Code states that only clerics may obtain the power of orders or of jurisdiction,[31] and since an ecclesiastical office in the strict sense must contain some participation in the power of orders or of jurisdiction,[32] it follows that only clerics may obtain an ecclesiastical office in the strict sense. In order that a person become a cleric, he must receive the first tonsure,[33] and by so doing he becomes incardinated in a diocese [34] and subject to the ordinary of the diocese.[35] From this fact the writer believes that a minor is exempt from the authority of his parents or tutors with reference to these things which are pertinent to his clerical state.

If dependence on the parents or tutors is claimed with reference to a renunciation of office, it must likewise be admitted for any other act which the cleric performs. Such an admission would place also the ordinary in a position of dependence on the parents or the tutors. It would certainly be an anomalous situation. A minor may act as plaintiff or respondent in a case involving spiritual things or things connected with the spiritual without the consent of his parents or guardians.[36] It seems that the same

---

30 Wernz-Vidal, *loc. cit.;* Coronata, *Institutiones,* I, n. 262.

31 Can. 118.

32 Can. 145, § 1.

33 Can. 108, § 1.

34 Can. 111, § 2.

35 Cans. 127–128.

36 Can. 1648, § 3.

liberty must be allowed him in the renunciation of an ecclesiastical office. Besides, before the Code any minor above the age of puberty could renounce an ecclesiastical office without any need of the consent of the parents or guardians.

It must be admitted that this discussion has little practical importance, for, while a cleric under the age of his majority may obtain an ecclesiastical office in the strict sense, it will be rare that such a cleric will have such an office conferred upon him. In most cases only priests will receive such offices, and since the age required for ordination to the priesthood is twenty-four years,[37] it is highly improbable that one will be ordained before the age of twenty-one years, even when a dispensation from the required age is granted.

SECTION 4. THE POWER OF THE ORDINARY TO ESTABLISH SPECIAL PROHIBITIONS

While the authors are in agreement on the point that a special prohibition with reference to the renunciation of an office may come from particular law,[38] they do not make any attempt to define the extent of the superior's power to enact such prohibitions. Could a bishop, for example, enact a diocesan statute prohibiting the renunciation of any and every office in the diocese even when according to the Code a just and proportionate cause is present to justify such a resignation? Or, can such a prohibition be enacted with reference only to a specific type of office or a specific group of offices, as, for example, the offices of the diocesan curia? Can such a prohibition be enacted as perpetual, or must it be of a temporary character suited to existing particular circumstances? The following discussion will be an attempt to propose an answer to these questions.

The general rule is that a bishop in his legislation may not prohibit anything which is expressly and undoubtedly permitted by common law, unless the common law clearly concedes him such power.[39] Canon 184 expressly permits anyone to renounce

---

[37] Can. 975.

[38] Maroto, *Institutiones,* I, n. 679; Blat, *Commentarium,* II, n. 131; Claeys Bouuaert-Simenon, *Manuale,* I, n. 340.

[39] Wernz-Vidal, *Ius Canonicum,* II, n. 599.

an ecclesiastical office if he is mentally capable of such an act and has a just cause for so doing. This general permission, however, is limited by the addition of a *nisi* clause which allows special prohibitions to be made in this regard. As has already been stated, these prohibitions may be derived from the common law or from particular law. It is certain, then, that the ordinary may prohibit the renunciation of an ecclesiastical office.

To what extent may the bishop make use of this power? The writer is of the opinion that the bishop may enact a prohibition affecting the renunciation of every office under his jurisdiction. Canon 184 itself makes no limitation in this regard. However, this does not mean that the writer concedes an arbitrary power to the bishop. A comparison of the present canon with canon 128 seems to clarify the bishop's position in the matter of establishing a prohibition against a resignation. This latter canon states that whenever and as long as in the judgment of the ordinary the needs of the Church demand it, unless there is a legitimate excusing impediment, clerics must accept and faithfully discharge any work assigned to them by the bishop. To the writer's mind these two canons consider the same problem from two different points of view. Canon 128 defines the circumstances in which a cleric must receive and retain an office, while canon 184 states the conditions under which the cleric may renounce an office. Canon 128, it is true, has reference to every type of charge that the bishop may impose upon a cleric, but offices in the strict sense are also included.[40]

The legitimate impediment mentioned in canon 128 is on a par with the just cause required by canon 184. Canon 128 mentions the "*necessitas Ecclesiae*" as the reason for permitting the ordinary to impose a charge on a cleric and to demand the faithful fulfillment of it. The words "*necessitas Ecclesiae*," to the writer's mind, are most important, and may be applied by analogy to canon 184 with reference to the imposition of a special prohibition against a resignation. In other words, the writer believes that the bishop may place a special prohibition against the resignation of a cleric when the needs of the Church demand

[40] Maroto, *Institutiones*, I, n. 553.

it. If the needs of the Church should demand it, then the ordinary could forbid the renunciation of any and every office in the diocese. Although canon 184 uses the phrase "*speciali prohibitione,*" this does not mean that the prohibition may be given only to an individual person or in reference to a specific office. Rather, it means that the prohibition, general or particular, is occasioned by special circumstances demanding such action. Such circumstances may be the result of a scarcity of competent priests in the diocese at a given time, or of a danger of schism which is threatening the diocese, or of any other similar and weighty consideration. The prohibition may extend only to the offices affected by such circumstances, and may be made operative only as long as the circumstances demand it. Otherwise the prohibition would be contrary to the freedom granted in canons 128 and 184. It is possible, however, that the circumstances may be of a perpetual nature, and therefore the prohibition may also be perpetual.

In brief, then, the ordinary may prohibit the renunciation of an ecclesiastical office or offices when the needs of the Church demand it. In reality, the prohibition is more or less simply a statement to the effect that a cause which under ordinary circumstances would justify a resignation is at present not in proportion to the needs of the Church. If there is doubt as to whether or not the prohibition is just, the cleric must obey, but he may institute a recourse to the Holy See *in devolutivo* against the prohibition.[41] The wording of the prohibition must be examined in each particular case in order to determine whether or not the prohibition affects the validity of the renunciation.[42]

---

[41] Coronata, *Institutiones,* I, n. 189.

[42] Claeys Bouuaert-Simenon, *Manuale,* I, p. 197, footnote 1.

CHAPTER VII

THE COMPETENT SUPERIOR FOR THE ADMISSION OF AN EXPRESS RENUNCIATION

Just as no ecclesiastical office may be obtained without the canonical provisionary intervention of the proper superior,[1] so also no ecclesiastical office may be renounced without the intervention of the proper ecclesiastical authority. This intervention of the proper superior may take place in either of two ways. In the majority of cases it is necessary for the validity of a resignation that it be presented to the competent superior and be accepted by him; in some cases, however, a mere presentation of the resignation to the proper superior offices.

Article I. The Generic Determination of the Competent Superior

> Canon 187, § 1. *Renuntiatio, generatim, ut valeat, ei fieri debet a quo est acceptanda, vel, si acceptatione non egeat, a quo clericus officium accepit vel qui eiusdem locum tenet.*
>
> § 2. *Quare si officium per confirmationem, admissionem, vel institutionem collatum fuerit, renuntiatio fieri debet superiori ad quem de iure ordinario confirmatio, admissio, vel institutio spectat.*

According to this canon it is generally required for the validity of a resignation that the resignation be presented to the competent superior. If the resignation needs to be accepted by the superior, then the superior by whom it is to be accepted is the one to whom it must be tendered. If, on the other hand, acceptance of the resignation by the superior is not required, then the resignation is to be tendered to the one from whom the office was received, or to the one who holds the place of that superior.

The Code gives no general rule for determining when a resig-

[1] Can. 147, § 1.

ation must be merely presented to a superior, and when it must also be accepted by him. Coronata is of the opinion that in general an office may be renounced by merely presenting the resignation to the superior when the office was conferred by means of a collative election. In other cases the acceptance of the resignation by the superior is required for the validity of the resignation.[2] This seems to be a safe rule to follow. The Code expressly mentions two cases in which a resignation need not be accepted by anyone, and both of these refer to offices which are conferred by a collative election, namely, the office of Roman Pontiff and the office of vicar capitular.[3]

Since the determination of the competent superior depends upon the source from which the incumbent receives the office, it is necessary to give a brief summary of the various modes in accordance with which the filling of ecclesiastical offices may be procured. The canonical assignment of office denotes the granting of an ecclesiastical office by the competent superior in accordance with the sacred canons.[4] This canonical assignment may be effected by an act of free conferral, of confirmation, of admission, of institution, or of collative election. An office is given by an act of free conferral when the superior both designates the person and grants the title to the office; by an act of confirmation on the part of the legitimate superior when the candidate has been designated by means of an election; by an act of admission on the part of the legitimate superior when the choice of the electors stands as an act of postulation, that is, when their election centers in one who is prevented from accepting the office by reason of an impediment from which a dispensation is customarily granted; by an act of institution when the candidate has been nominated or presented by another; by an act of collative election when the election itself designates the person and confers the title to the office.

In all of these cases, with one exception, the competent superior for the admission of the resignation is the person who in his own right has freely conferred the office or who by ordinary title and

[2] *Institutiones,* I, n. 263.

[3] Can. 221; 443, § 1.

[4] Can. 147, § 2.

right has bestowed the required confirmation, institution or admission to the office. The ones who elect, present, nominate or postulate the candidate retain no right to participate in the renunciation of the office. The one exception is the case of collative election. Since in this case no confirmation is necessary, the resignation must be presented to the body of electors who conferred the office. As has already been stated, the acceptance of the resignation by the body of electors is not required as a general rule.

It is to be noted that canon 187, § 2, states that the resignation must be tendered to the superior who has the power of confirmation, institution or admission to the office by ordinary right. The purpose of this paragraph is to indicate that the persons who elect, nominate, present or postulate a candidate do not retain any right to participate in the renunciation of the office, but it serves also to emphasize the fact that the superior who is to participate in the renunciation of the office is the one who by ordinary right has the power of confirmation, institution or admission to the office. The same principle holds also for the renunciation of an office which is obtained by an act of free conferral or collative election. This principle is clearly enunciated in canon 158, which reads as follows:

> *Qui, alius negligentiam vel impotentiam supplens, officium confert, nullam inde potestatem acquirit in nominatum; sed huius iuridicus status perinde constituitur, ac si provisio ad ordinariam iuris normam peracta fuisset.*

Hence, if, for example, the metropolitan, by supplying the negligence of a suffragan bishop, has instituted in office a person presented by a patron in the suffragan diocese,[5] the suffragan bishop, and not the metropolitan, is the competent superior for the acceptance of the renunciation of that office. In the same manner the cathedral chapter and the diocesan consultors are the ones to whom the vicar capitular and the diocesan administrator must tender their resignation, even though they had been appointed to their office by the metropolitan because of the chapter's or the consultors' failure to act within the time specified

[5] Can. 274, § 1.

by the law.[6] In both of these instances the metropolitan actually confers the office, but only by reason of a devolved right, and hence the resignation must be presented to the one who by ordinary right should have conferred the office.[7]

Thus the competent superior for the admission of the renunciation of an office is the superior who by ordinary right has the power to confer the office in any of the ways enumerated above. It is not necessary that, in order to be competent to receive the resignation, the superior also have the power of removing the incumbent from the office. Before the Code some authors proposed the contrary as at least a probable opinion.[8] Canon 187 does not mention this power as being necessary, and, besides, canon 193, § 1, in speaking of the superior who is competent to transfer a cleric from one office to another, states that the superior must have the power both of accepting the resignation of the first office and of removing the incumbent from the first office, as well as the power of promoting the cleric to the other office. From this canon it appears evident that the power of removing a cleric from an office is not necessarily pre-required for the power of accepting his resignation from the office.

Canon 187, § 1 likewise states that the person who holds the superior's place is also competent to accept the resignation. Blat remarks that the person may be either the competent superior's successor, or a person delegated for accepting a particular resignation by the superior.[9]

The participation of the competent superior in the act of renunciation of office is required for the validity of the resignation, whether his participation be merely passive in that the resignation must at least be presented to him, or whether it be also active in that he must positively furnish his acceptance of the resignation.

The adverb "*generatim,*" as contained in the wording of canon

---

[6] Can. 432, § 2.

[7] Chelodi, *Ius de Personis* (ed. altera a Sac. Ernest Bertagnolli, Tridenti: Libr. Edit. Tridentum, 1927), n. 147.

[8] *Glos. Ord.* ad. c. un., *de renuntiatione,* I, 4, in Clem., s.v., *manibus;* Pirhing, *Jus Canonicum,* lib. I, tit. IX, n. LXIX.

[9] *Commentarium,* I, n. 134.

187, § 1, has received different interpretations from the authors. Some authors apply it exclusively to the first part of the paragraph of this canon, in which mention is made of a resignation which requires the acceptance of the superior for its validity.[10] Thus these authors consider the adverb as serving notice that not all resignations need to be accepted by the superior for the validity of the resignation. They point to the resignation of the Pope and the vicar capitular as examples of resignations which need only to be presented without the additional requirement that they need also to be accepted by someone.

Other authors consider "*generatim*" as having reference to the entire first paragraph of canon 187, and thus they look upon it as leaving room for an exceptional kind of resignation in which neither the presentation of it to a superior nor the acceptance of it by a superior is required for the validity of the resignation.[11] These authors consider the resignation of the Pope as the only example of such an exceptional kind of resignation.

The latter opinion seems to the writer to be more in agreement with the structure of the sentence in canon 187, § 1. The adverb is so placed as to indicate that it modifies the principal verb of the sentence without any special reference to either of the dependent clauses. It seems rather to qualify the content of the whole paragraph, and thus seems to make allowance for a case in which a resignation may be made even without the necessity of its being presented to anyone.

Since the resignation of the Roman Pontiff is the only resignation of this type, the divergent opinions affect the manner of only his resignation. The authors who contend that the resignation of the Roman Pontiff is to be presented to the College of Cardinals do not state whether they regard this presentation as a requirement for the validity of the resignation. If the general

---

[10] Augustine, *A Commentary,* II, 158; Blat, *Commentarium,* I, n. 134; Beste, *Introductio in Codicem* (ed. altera, Collegeville, Minn.: St. John's Abbey Press, 1944), p. 210.

[11] Coronata, *Institutiones,* I, p. 302, footnote 8; Toso, *Ad Codicem Iuris Canonici Commentaria Minora* (5 vols., Vol. II, 1921, Romae: Marietti), II, 153 (Hereafter this work is cited as *Commentaria Minora*); Maroto, Institutiones, I, n. 682.

rule should apply, it should be regarded as necessary for the validity if it is required at all. Canon 221 states that the resignation of the Roman Pontiff need not be accepted by anyone in order that it be valid. The same canon does not state whether the presentation of the resignation to the College of Cardinals is or is not necessary.

Most of the authors maintain that the resignation of the Pope may be communicated to the public in any way that he wishes.[12] This view is more in conformity with the fact of the Pope's supremacy in the Church, and also with the words of Pope Boniface VIII in this regard: ". . . Romanum Pontificem posse libere resignare."[13] Hence, even though one accepts the interpretation of the first group of authors and correspondingly classifies the resignation of the Pope as one which is to be presented to the College of Cardinals, one may not, so it appears, insist that on the part of the Pope the presentation of his resignation to the College of Cardinals is a requirement for the validity of his resignation.

The laity are excluded from any competence in the matter of admitting the renunciation of an office. As a matter of fact, if a cleric presumes to resign an office, benefice or dignity in the hands of a lay person, he automatically incurs a censure of suspension *a divinis*.[14] This suspension forbids the exercise of any act of orders, whether such power be possessed by reason of ordination or through a privilege.[15] Since canon 2400, which enacts the penalty, contains the word "*praesumpserit,*" any reduction of imputability in the act excuses the cleric from incurring the censure.[16] The resignation, however, is invalid by reason of canon 187, which in its nature of an invalidating law requires a competent superior for the valid acceptance of a resignation.

---

[12] Coronata, *op. cit.*, n. 316; Maroto, *loc. cit.;* Toso, *loc. cit.;* Augustine, *A Commentary,* II, p. 210; Chelodi, *Jus de Personis,* n. 147.

[13] C. 1, *de renuntiatione,* I, 7, in VIo.

[14] Can. 2400.

[15] Can. 2279, § 2, n. 2.

[16] Can. 2229, § 2.

ARTICLE II. THE SPECIFIC DETERMINATION OF THE COMPETENT SUPERIOR

Subsequent to the discussion concerning the generic determination of the competent superior for the acceptance of a resignation according to the prescriptions of canon 187 an attempt will be made to enumerate the more important competent superiors and the respective offices for the resignation of which they are competent. The writer makes no pretense at presenting a complete list either of the competent superiors or of the respective offices. Such an endeavor would connote a vast undertaking which unnecessarily, and even uselessly, would take the writer far afield in the prosecution of the present study. The general rules formulated above will be applied to the more important superiors with an indication of the extent of the superior's power. Unless mention is made to the contrary, the reader should assume that the resignation under consideration must not only be presented to, but also be accepted by, the superior who is designated as the competent superior.

SECTION 1. THE ROMAN PONTIFF

By reason of his supremacy and plenitude of power in the Church [17] the Roman Pontiff may execute the conferral of any and every kind of office in the Church if he sees fit to do so. For the same reason he may reserve to himself the right to accept the renunciation of any given office in the Church. Likewise, any incumbent of an ecclesiastical office may make a valid resignation in the hands of the Roman Pontiff if he wishes to do so and if the Pope is willing to take the place of the lower competent superior in accepting the resignation. Such a case may occur if the lower competent superior refuses to accept a resignation, or does not act upon a resignation within the time prescribed in canon 189.[18]

If the Pope or his delegate accepts the resignation from a benefice, then the conferral of the benefice for that time is reserved to the Pope.[19] If, however, the benefice is a manual benefice or one

[17] Can. 218, § 1.

[18] Haydt, *Reserved Benefices,* p. 100.

[19] Can. 1435, § 1, n. 4.

of mixed or of lay patronage, then express mention must be made of the fact of reservation with reference to the conferral of the benefice. Otherwise it is not reserved even though the Pope accepts the resignation.[20] It is to be noted that this reservation takes place only when a benefice is renounced in the hands of the Pope or of his delegate. An office which is not a benefice is not included under the prescriptions of canon 1435.

Although the Pope is competent both for the conferral of all offices in the Church and for the acceptance of the resignation of the same, the number of cases in which he actually exercises this power is comparatively small. In general one may say that the Pope confers the major offices in the Church. A major office is one that partakes of episcopal or quasi-episcopal power.[21] Thus cardinals,[22] apostolic legates,[23] patriarchs and primates,[24] archbishops,[25] bishops,[26] coadjutor and auxiliary bishops,[27] vicars and prefects apostolic,[28] apostolic administrators[29] and abbots and prelates *nullius*[30] are all appointed by the Holy See and must tender their resignation to the Roman Pontiff. Express mention of the Pope's competency in this matter is made with reference to the resignation of a residential bishop and of an apostolic legate.[31] The Pope's exclusive competency with reference to the other offices is deduced from the fact that he is the superior competent to confer such offices.

The conferral of the dignities in the chapter of a cathedral or a collegiate church is also reserved to the Holy See.[32] A dignity is an

20 Can. 1435, § 2.

21 Sipos, *Enchiridion Iuris Canonici* (3. ed., Pécs: Ex Typographia "Haladás R. T.," 1936), p. 143. Hereafter this work is cited as *Enchiridion*.

22 Can. 232, § 1.

23 Can. 265.

24 Can. 271.

25 Can. 272.

26 Can. 329, § 2.

27 Can. 350, § 1.

28 Can. 293, § 1.

29 Can. 312.

30 Can. 320, § 1.

31 Can. 350, § 1; 268, § 2.

32 Can. 396, § 1.

office in the chapter which has some prerogative of honor attached to it.[33] According to the rule of canon 187, then, the resignation of these dignities must be made to the Holy See, since the Holy See is the one who confers them.

Likewise the major officials of the Roman Curia must tender their resignation to the Roman Pontiff, since they too are freely appointed by the Pope.[34] In general the major officials of the Roman Curia are the prefects, secretaries, sub-secretaries and assessors. In the Sacred Roman Rota the major officials are the ten auditors, the promoter of justice and the defender of the bond.[35]

Regarding all the offices thus far mentioned the resignation must be made in the hands of the Roman Pontiff or of someone delegated by him, since these offices are conferred either by him personally or on his authority. There is, however, another kind of resignation which can be accepted only by the Roman Pontiff, not because of the fact that he conferred the office, but because of the special prescription of the Code in its regard. Canon 1486 forbids the ordinary to accept the resignation of a benefice in favor of another or with a condition affecting the subsequent conferral of the benefice or the distribution of the fruits of the benefice. Hence such conditional resignations must be made to the Pope. The ordinary may, however, accept the resignation of a benefice in favor of another when the benefice is under litigation and one of the contesting parties cedes it in favor of the other litigant. Likewise the ordinary may accept the resignation of a pastor with the reservation of a pension for the lifetime of the pensioner chargeable to the benefice in favor of the resigning pastor, provided that the pension does not exceed one-third of the net revenue of the benefice.[36]

---

[33] Vermeersch-Creusen, *Epitome*, I, n. 497.

[34] *Ordo servandus in Sacris Congregationibus, Tribunalibus, Officiis Romanae Curiae: Pars Prima, Normae Communes,* 29 iun. 1908, c. I, n. 1—*AAS,* I (1909), 37; Pius XI, Const. "*Ad incrementum decoris,*" 15 aug. 1934—*AAS,* XXVI (1934), 503; 504–505; 509; 512–513; 516–517; 519.

[35] *Lex Propria Sacrae Romanae Rotae et Signaturae Apostolicae,* 29 iun. 1908, c. I, 4—*AAS,* I (1909), 20–21; *Normae S. Romanae Rotae Tribunalis,* 29 iun. 1934—*AAS,* XXVI (1934), 451.

[36] P. C. I., 20 maii 1923, ad IX—*AAS,* XVI (1924), 116.

One may think it strange that nothing has been said with reference to canon 1435, which contains an exhaustive list of the benefices the conferral of which is reserved to the Holy See. A brief examination of this canon will demonstrate that the matter of resignation is affected very little by these reservations. The canon reads as follows:

> §1. *Praeter omnia beneficia consistorialia et omnes dignitates ecclesiarum cathedralium et collegiatarum ad normam can. 396, § 1, sunt reservata Sedi Apostolicae, quanquam vacanti, sola beneficia quae infra memorantur:*
> 1°. *Omnia beneficia, etiam curata, quae vacaverint per obitum, promotionem, renuntiationem vel translationem S.R.E. Cardinalium, Legatorum Romani Pontificis, officialium maiorum Sacrarum Congregationum, Tribunalium, et Officiorum Romanae Curiae et Familiarium, etiam honoris tantum, Summi Pontificis tempore vacationis beneficii;*
> 2°. *Quae, fundata extra Romanam Curiam, vacaverint per beneficiarii obitum in ipsa Urbe;*
> 3°. *Quae invalide ob simoniae vitium collata fuerint;*
> 4°. *Denique beneficia quibus Romanus Pontifex per se vel per delegatum manus apposuit his quae sequuntur modis; si electionem ad beneficium irritam declaraverit; vel vetuerit ad electionem procedere; si renuntiationem admiserit; si beneficiarium promoverit, transtulerit, beneficio privaverit; si beneficium in commendam dederit.*

At first glance one would perhaps conclude that these benefices must be renounced in the hands of the Pope, since the conferral of them is reserved to the Holy See. However, such is not the case. Haydt explains well the nature of these reservations.[37] He states that only a real reservation is perpetual in its effects; all other types of reservation cease as soon as the superior to whom the benefice is reserved has conferred the benefice. A real reservation is one that reserves a benefice because of some element proper to the benefice itself. The only real reservations in the Code are the reservation of consistorial benefices and the reservation of dignities in the chapter of cathedral and collegiate churches. Hence only these benefices remain reserved after the Pope has conferred them,

[37] *Reserved Benefices*, pp. 78–81.

and therefore it is only regarding them that the resignation must be made in the hands of the Pope. The other benefices, mentioned in nn. 1–4 of canon 1435, are to be renounced in the hands of the superior who has the ordinary right to confer them. If this were not so, then the benefices mentioned in nn. 1–4 of canon 1435 could never revert to the ordinary collator in the matter of their conferral, for, if the Roman Pontiff had to accept the resignation of them, the subsequent conferral of them would be reserved once more by reason of n. 4 of this canon. Such is obviously not the intention of the legislator.

Since the resignation of consistorial benefices and of dignities in chapters of cathedral and collegiate churches has already been considered, canon 1435 adds for notice here no new benefices to the list of those which must be renounced in the hands of the Roman Pontiff or his delegate.

SECTION 2. THE LOCAL ORDINARY

Can. 152. *Loci Ordinarius ius habet providendi officiis ecclesiasticis in proprio territorio, nisi aliud probetur; hac tamen potestate caret Vicarius Generalis sine mandato speciali.*

Can 1432, § 1. *Ad collationem beneficiorum vacantium, Cardinalis in proprio titulo vel diaconia et Ordinarius loci in proprio territorio habent intentionem in iure fundatam.*

§ 2. *Conferre autem beneficia nequit Vicarius Generalis sine speciali mandato; Vicarius autem Capitularis nec paroecias vacantes, nisi ad normam can. 455, § 2, n. 3, neque alia beneficia perpetua liberae collationis.*

After the Roman Pontiff the superior who holds a prominent position with reference to offices and benefices is the local ordinary. This position is clearly stated in the canons quoted above. From these canons there is established a presumption in favor of the right of the local ordinary to confer offices and benefices. From this presumption there arises another presumption in favor of the local ordinary, namely, a presumption in favor of his right to accept the renunciation of all offices and benefices in his territory. Naturally these rights may be limited and are limited by any reservations that the Pope sees fit to make.

It remains now to determine who are the local ordinaries and what is the extent of their power. According to canon 198, §§ 1–2, the following persons are included under the term "local ordinary": residential bishops, abbots and prelates *nullius* and their vicars general, administrators, vicars and prefects apostolic and all those who succeed the aforementioned ordinaries in the rule of their territory. With but few exceptions all the local ordinaries obtain the rights of a residential bishop in their territory, and, like residential bishops, are competent for the conferral and for the acceptance of the renunciation of all offices in their territory. Thus vicars and prefects apostolic,[38] pro-vicars and pro-prefects apostolic,[39] abbots and prelates *nullius*,[40] permanent apostolic administrators [41] and coadjutor bishops who are given to a totally incapacitated bishop [42] enjoy the rights of a residential bishop, and like him may confer offices and benefices in the territory, and also may receive the resignation of the incumbent of any office or benefice.

The vicar capitular or, in places where there is no cathedral chapter, the diocesan administrator, who rules the see when it is vacant or impeded, is also a local ordinary, but does not enjoy the fulness of power in this matter that the local ordinaries already enumerated enjoy. He enjoys the same ordinary power as the bishop in spiritual and temporal matters in all things which are not expressly forbidden to him by the law.[43] He is expressly forbidden to confer parishes of free conferral until the see has been vacant for a year,[44] and is also forbidden to confer perpetual

---

[38] Can. 294, § 1; cf. Winslow, *Vicars and Prefects Apostolic*, The Catholic University of America Canon Law Studies, n. 24 (Washington, D. C.: The Catholic University of America, 1924), pp. 15–30.

[39] Can. 309, § 2; 310, § 2.

[40] Can. 323, § 1; cf. Benko, *The Abbot Nullius*, The Catholic University of America Canon Law Studies, n. 173 (Washington, D. C.: The Catholic University of America Press, 1943), pp. 87–100.

[41] Can. 315, § 1; cf. McDonough, *Apostolic Administrators*, The Catholic University of America Canon Law Studies, n. 139 (Washington, D. C.: The Catholic University of America Press, 1941), pp. 158–166.

[42] Can. 351, § 2.

[43] Can. 435, § 1.

[44] Can. 455, § 2, n. 3.

benefices of free conferral.[45] Since he is expressly forbidden to confer these benefices, it is to be concluded then that he is likewise incompetent to receive the renunciation of persons who possess them, for he does not hold the place of the bishop in these things.

Since these are the only two express prohibitions in the Code, it seems logical to conclude that the vicar capitular is competent to receive the renunciation of all other offices in the territory. It is to be noted that the limitations of his power have reference only to offices which are at the same time benefices. Canon 426, § 5, expresses the competency of the vicar capitular with reference to the resignation of a diocesan consultor. The canon states that if a diocesan consultor dies or resigns while the see is vacant, then the vicar capitular is to name another consultor to fill his place with the consent of the remaining consultors. Since the canon mentions the possibility for a resignation to be made by a diocesan consultor during the vacancy of the see, it is postulated then that the vicar capitular must be capable of accepting such a resignation, since he alone has charge of the see at the time.

The writer is of the opinion that the vicar capitular can confer all the offices in the diocese with the exception of the two types of benefices already mentioned, and can also accept the resignation of the incumbents of these offices. It is necessary to establish the vicar capitular's right to confer these offices in order to permit him to accept the renunciation of them, for, in the present law, the right of conferral and the right of accepting resignations are correlative rights. If it is not admitted that these rights are correlative, then it must be admitted that the vicar general has the power to accept the resignation of any office in the diocese, since the Code does not require a special mandate for the vicar general with reference to the acceptance of resignations from offices, but requires it only with reference to the conferral of offices. No one grants the vicar general such power.

In the pre-Code law there was no canon or decree which stated that the competent superior for the acceptance of a resignation was the superior who had the right to confer the office or benefice. The lack of a definite provision in this matter gave rise to a

---

[45] Can. 1432, § 2.

dispute among the authors as to the power of the chapter to accept resignations when the see was vacant. By law the chapter could not confer benefices which pertained to the free conferral of the bishop when the see was vacant, but it could grant institution to a candidate who was presented for a benefice by a patron.[46]

Some authors maintained that the chapter could accept the resignation of only those benefices which it could confer.[47] These authors applied the principle that one could receive the resignation of only those offices which he had the power to confer. They deduced this principle from the laws which were in existence with reference to the resignation of specific offices. Other authors held that the chapter could accept the resignation of even those offices which pertained to the bishop alone for their conferral.[48] These authors considered that, since the chapter received the full power of the bishop except in those things which were expressly forbidden to it, it could therefore receive the resignation of all offices inasmuch as there was no express prohibition to the contrary. In other words, these authors consider that a limitation upon the power of conferring benefices did not imply a limitation upon the power of accepting resignations.

The opinion of the earlier-mentioned group of authors has been adopted in the Code in canon 187. Thus one may receive the resignation of only those offices which he has the power to confer. As has already been stated, the writer is of the opinion that the vicar capitular can confer all offices in the territory with the exception of the two types of benefices already mentioned, and therefore he can likewise accept the resignations which are tendered from these offices.

The authors are quite vague in their determination of the

---

[46] C. 2, X, *ne sede vacante aliquid innovetur,* III, 9; Potthast, n. 7794; c. 1, *de institutionibus,* III, 6, in VI°.

[47] Pirhing, *Jus Canonicum,* lib. I, tit. IX, n. 74; Reiffenstuel, *Jus Canonicum,* lib. I, tit. IX, n. 7; Santi, *Praelectiones,* lib. I, tit. IX, n. 20; "Traité des Résignations"—*Analecta Iuris Pontificii* (Romae, 1855–1869; Parisiis, 1872–1891), II (1857), 1522.

[48] Garcia, *Tractatus de Beneficiis,* pars XI, c. III, n. 260; Leurenius, *Forum Beneficiale,* pars III, c. 714; Schmalzgrueber, *Jus Ecclesiasticum,* lib. I, tit. IX, n. 22; Gillmann, "Die Resignation der Benefizien"—*AKKR,* LXXX (1900), 543.

power of the vicar capitular with reference to the conferral of offices. For the most part they restrict themselves to a considera-tion of the powers which are expressly mentioned in the Code.[49] It would not be fair to state that these authors exclude the vicar capitular from competency in the conferral of offices except for the few cases in which the Code explicitly confirms his com-petency. However, they do fail to mention that he has the right in other cases. Chelodi (1880–1922) [50] and Cappello,[51] on the other hand, expressly state that the vicar capitular can confer offices only in the few cases in which the Code explicitly mentions his competency.

Since, however, the chapter and the vicar capitular receive all the ordinary jurisdiction of the bishop except in those things which are expressly forbidden to them by law,[52] and since there is no general prohibition on the Code by which they are for-bidden to confer offices, they must be considered as competent in all cases in which the law does not expressly exclude them from competency. It follows from this that they may also accept the resignation from offices in all these cases, since the two powers are correlative. The exceptional cases have already been stated, namely, perpetual benefices of free conferral and parishes of free conferral. The latter type of benefices ceases to be an exception when the see has been vacant for a year.

Another local ordinary is the temporary apostolic administrator. Such an apostolic administrator is appointed to rule a see either *sede vacante* or *sede plena.* He has the same rights as the vicar

---

[49] Cocchi, *Commentarium,* II, n. 67; Coronata, *Institutiones,* I, p. 244, footnote 4; Castillo, *Disertacion Historico-Canonico sobre la Podestad del Cabildo en Sede Vacante o Impedida del Vicario Capitular,* The Catholic University of America Canon Law Studies, n. 4 (Washington, D. C.: The Catholic University of America, 1919), pp. 76–83; Klekotka, *Diocesan Con-sultors,* The Catholic University of America Canon Law Studies, n. 8 (Washington, D. C.: The Catholic University of America, 1920), pp. 157–159; McDonough, *Apostolic Administrators,* pp. 145–149.

[50] *Ius de Personis,* n. 147.

[51] *Summa Iuris Canonici* (3 vols., Vol. I, 3. ed., Romae: Apud Aedes Universitatis Gregorianae, 1938), n. 281.

[52] Can. 435, § 1.

capitular.[53] However, a distinction must be made between the temporary apostolic administrator who is appointed to a vacant see and the one who is appointed to a see which is still occupied. The former, like the vicar capitular, can not confer parochial benefices of free conferral within the first year of the vacancy of the see; the latter, who is appointed to a see which is still occupied, can confer such benefices from the moment that he assumes the administration of the diocese, unless his letter of appointment states otherwise.[54] Hence the power of the temporary apostolic administrator who is appointed to a vacant see has the same power as the vicar capitular with reference to the acceptance of renunciations of office; the power of the temporary apostolic administrator appointed to a see which is still occupied extends beyond that power, for he may admit the resignation of parochial benefices of free conferral from the time he enters upon the office.

Finally, the vicar general is also a local ordinary, but, since he can not confer an ecclesiastical office or benefice without a special mandate,[55] he is likewise incompetent for accepting the renunciation of an ecclesiastical office without a special mandate.[56] Augustine (1872–1943) requires a special mandate for the conferral of each specific office,[57] but, as Coronata notes,[58] this interpretation is too severe and is not demanded by the canon. The special mandate could extend to the conferral of all offices in the territory. In the same manner a special mandate may be given to the vicar general to authorize him to accept the resignation of any office in the territory. It is to be noted that a special mandate empowering the vicar general with the conferral of offices does not concede to him the right to accept the resignations of those offices. If nothing is said with reference to the acceptance of the resignations, then it seems that the general rule should

[53] Can. 315, § 2, n. 1.

[54] For a thorough discussion of this point, cf. McDonough, *Apostolic Administrators*, pp. 136–149.

[55] Can. 152; 1432, § 2.

[56] Campagna, *Il Vicario Generale del Vescovo*, The Catholic University of America Canon Law Studies, n. 66 (Washington, D. C.: The Catholic University of America, 1931), p. 130.

[57] *A Commentary*, II, 110.

[58] *Institutiones*, I, p. 244, footnote 3.

hold, namely, that the resignation be presented to the superior who by ordinary right confers the office. The vicar general in this case is an extraordinary collator, and unless he has a special mandate for the acceptance of the resignation, it seems that he is not qualified to take the place of the bishop in this regard.

SECTION 3. CARDINALS

If a cardinal is at the same time a residential bishop, then there can be no question with reference to his competency for the acceptance of renunciations of office in his territory. He is in such a case a local ordinary with all the rights of a residential bishop. This is expressly mentioned in the Code with reference to cardinal bishops and their suburbicarian sees,[59] but it is true also of any cardinal who resides outside the Roman Curia in the capacity of a diocesan bishop.

Cardinal priests and cardinal deacons have an "*intentionem in iure fundatam*" with reference to the conferral of benefices in their respective title churches and deaconries.[60] Thus one must neutralize the operative effect of this claim as founded in the law in order to vindicate for himself any right in the conferral of these benefices. The cardinal, however, must be present in the Roman Curia in order to exercise this right of conferral. This had been the practice of the Roman Curia, and is now confirmed by a recent response of the Sacred Congregation of the Council, which stated that when the cardinal titulars are absent from Rome the conferral of the vacant benefices in their churches is reserved to the Holy See according to the norms of canon 1435, § 3.[61] Except for the case, then, in which a cardinal is not resident in Rome, he possesses the right to confer the benefices in his titular church and also the right to accept the resignation of the incumbents of these benefices.

---

59 Can. 240, § 1.

60 Can. 1432, § 1.

61 12 iun. 1943—*AAS*, XXXV (1943), 339—*The Jurist* (Washington, D. C., 1941-), IV (1944), 630-632.

CHAPTER VIII

THE FREEDOM REQUIRED IN AN EXPRESS RENUNCIATION

> Canon 185. *Renuntiatio ex metu gravi, iniuste incusso, dolo aut errore substantiali vel simoniace facta, irrita est ipso iure.*

The renunciation of an ecclesiastical office, like other juridical acts, may be influenced by various vitiating elements. The legislator has taken cognizance of this fact by providing a special canon with reference to the effects that these elements have upon a resignation. In commenting upon this canon authors apply its prescriptions only to the act of resignation as it is placed by the incumbent.[1] Only when speaking of simony do they mention the superior's act of acceptance as coming under the prescriptions of this canon. The writer believes that this interpretation, which the authors give at least by implication, is unwarranted. If the acceptance of the resignation by the superior is required for the validity of a resignation, as it is in almost every renunciation of office, then the writer believes that the resignation is invalid if the superior's act of acceptance is interfered with in the manner described in canon 185.

This opinion is based upon the interpretation of the phrase "*renuntiatio . . . facta*" as contained in canon 185. This phrase is general and therefore can quite naturally represent the complete act of resignation, inclusive of the acceptance of the resignation by the superior. Substantially the same phrase is used in canon 191, § 1, which reads as follows:

> *Semel legitime facta renuntiatione, non datur amplius poenitentiae locus, licet renuntians possit officium ex alio titulo consequi.*

[1] Maroto, *Institutiones,* I, n. 680; Cocchi, *Commentarium,* II, n. 98; Claeys Bouuaert-Simenon, *Manuale,* I, n. 340; Coronata, *Institutiones,* I, n. 263.

The Pontifical Commission for the Interpretation of the Code in response to a question proposed concerning this canon stated that a person may withdraw his resignation provided that he does so before the superior has accepted it.[2] This response forces one to conclude that the phrase "*legitime facta renuntiatione,*" as contained in canon 191, § 1, implies the completed act of resignation, which includes the acceptance of the resignation by the superior. Mannucci, in commenting upon this response, stated that possibly the word "*legitime*" was the key to the solution, since a resignation could not be considered legitimately complete until the acceptance of the superior had taken place.[3] This explanation is not conclusive, but even if it were, one could hardly expect the use of the term "*legitime*" in canon 185, where the law speaks of the effect that grave fear and other elements have upon the validity of a resignation.

The writer believes that the phrase in canon 185 is substantially the same as the one used in canon 191, § 1, and should therefore receive the same interpretation, namely, that it includes the act of the incumbent and the act of the superior when it is required that the superior accept the resignation. If this interpretation is not accepted, then the superior's act of acceptance of a resignation, if vitiated by fear, deceit, or error, must be judged according to the general norms established in the Code for determining the effect that these elements have upon a juridical act.

No difficulty would be encountered with reference to error, since the general norm in canon 104 is in its import identical with the prescriptions of canon 185. On the other hand, with reference to grave fear and deceit, some difficulty of interpretation would surely be occasioned. Canon 103, § 2 states that acts placed under the influence of unjustly inspired grave fear and deceit are valid unless the law decrees otherwise. Such acts may be rescinded by the sentence of the judge acting either at the request of the injured party or by reason of his office. Canon 185 takes exception to this rule by declaring that a renunciation of office made under the influence of unjustly inspired grave fear or under the

[2] 14 iul. 1922, ad III—*AAS,* XIV (1922), 527.

[3] *Il Monitore Ecclesiastico* (Romae, 1876–), serie IV, Vol. II (Vol. XXIV della intera collezione) (1922), 340–341.

prevalence of deceit, is invalid. If the superior's act of acceptance of the resignation is not included under the prescriptions of canon 185, then, if grave fear or deceit influence the act of acceptance, the resignation is valid but rescissible according to the general rule. This places the superior at a distinct disadvantage, for he must make use of a judicial sentence in order to rescind the renunciation. But it appears evident that it is the precise purpose of the special prescriptions of canon 185 to give greater protection to the renunciation of an office than to other juridical acts in general.

The writer fails to see why the legislator would protect the incumbent from injury to his rights without granting the same protection to the superior. This conclusion appears all the more convincing when one considers that the use of grave fear or deceit upon the superior would inflict not only a personal injury, but rather also a social one by causing a detrimental reaction with reference to general discipline and respect for authority. It is true that the superior could obviate the ensuing difficulty by conferring the office on the cleric anew, but the fact remains that the accepted resignation on the part of the superior who acted under the duress of an unjustly inspired grave fear, or under the influence of deceit, would stand as binding with valid effect in the face of the moral pressure which induced the superior to act. Such recognition in law appears not only questionable, but indefensible as well.

Accordingly, in the following pages everything that is stated with reference to the interpretation of canon 185 must be applied in equal manner to both the act of resignation of the incumbent and to the act of acceptance of the superior.

Article I. Freedom from Force and Fear

Section 1. Freedom from Force

Although canon 185 makes no specific mention of force or violence, it seems fitting to say a few words concerning this element, especially since it is so closely related to the element of fear. Force may be defined as the impact of outward violence employed by an external agent to compel another to do what is contrary to his will. Force is distinguished as physical or moral. Physical force is present when the violence coming from the external agent is of such intensity that it can not be repulsed, while at the same time the one suffering the violence is entirely opposed to his enforced act. Moral force, on the other hand, is present when a person either does not resist as much as he should or does not entirely dissent internally to the act which he is compelled to perform.

Canon 103, § 1, states that when the acts of physical or moral persons are placed under the influence of an external force which cannot be repulsed, they are considered as not having been placed by the person. This canon is merely a restatement of the natural law, which requires the participation of the will in a human act. Hence, a renunciation of an ecclesiastical office effected under the influence of physical force is invalid. Such would be the case if, for example, an incumbent of an office were forced in this way to affix his signature to a document containing a statement to the effect that he was renouncing his office.

No provision is made with reference to the effect that moral force has upon a juridical act. Authors, however, consider that moral force most frequently gives rise to fear, and for this reason the principles regarding fear are to be applied to it.[4]

SECTION 2. FREEDOM FROM GRAVE FEAR

Fear is defined as a disturbance of the mind caused by the apprehension of an imminent or future evil.[5] The evil that is apprehended may be either of a physical or of a moral nature. Hence the threat of the loss of life, of bodily injury, or the loss of one's good name, or of a financial loss may constitute a source of fear. The evil need not threaten the individual personally; it may threaten some one who is attached to him by

---

[4] Cf. Cocchi, *Commentarium,* II, n. 10; Cappello, *Tractatus Canonico-Moralis de Sacramentis* (3 vols., Vol. III, *De Matrimonio,* 3. ed., 1933, Taurinorum Augustae: Marietti), III, n. 603; Claeys Bouuaert-Simenon, *Manuale,* I, n. 256.

[5] Noldin-Schmitt, *Summa Theologiae Moralis* (3 vols., Vol. I, 27. ed., 1940, Oeniponte: Rauch), I, n. 54. The general remarks on fear, its divisions, etc., are taken from this work.

reason of a particular bond, as, for example, the bond of blood or of friendship.

Fear is divided into grave fear and slight fear, depending upon whether the threatening evil is of a grave or of a slight nature. In order that the fear be considered grave, the evil must be grave and also difficult to avert. The fear is absolutely grave when the evil which threatens is sufficient to arouse grave fear in even a resolute person; it is relatively grave when the evil, in itself insufficient to cause grave fear in an ordinary person, arouses grave fear in a certain individual by reason of the particular circumstance of age, of sex, or of some other factor. On the other hand, fear is slight when the evil is neither absolutely nor relatively grave, or when the evil of whatsoever gravity it may be can be easily averted.

Fear is also distinguished as internal or external. The former arises from a cause which is not dependent on a free agent, as, for example, from a storm or from sickness; the latter is inspired by a free agent. Since this fear is inspired by a free agent, it may be a just or unjust fear. It is just if the person who inspires it has the right to do so and does it in the proper manner. Thus, a judge has the right to inspire fear in a culprit by threatening a penalty which is provided in the law. The fear is unjust if the person who inspires it has no genuine claim in support of his action, or if he presses unduly or excessively whatever rightful claim he has.

Another type of fear usually considered by the authors is reverential fear. This fear arises from the dread of offending or giving pain to those whom a person should respect or love. This fear may also be just or unjust according to the rule already given. Ordinarily reverential fear is only a slight fear. It may, however, be grave because of concomitant factors such as the dread of harsh treatment or of continual remonstrances from the superior.

Canon 185, taking exception to the general rule on grave fear as contained in canon 103, § 2, states that a renunciation of office is invalid if made under the influence of an unjustly inspired grave fear. The fear in this case must be grave. Both absolutely grave and relatively grave fear produce the same effect.

Besides, the fear must be unjustly inspired in the individual by a person whose act is not properly warranted, or if warranted, not properly executed. If a superior, for example, should effect a resignation by threatening a penalty on the incumbent, the resignation would be null if the penalty was one which the law does not permit him to inflict upon anyone. On the other hand, the resignation would be valid if the fear arose from the threat of a just and licit penalty. The Sacred Congregation of the Council upheld the validity of a resignation which was made through fear of a trial that was being instituted against the incumbent for a crime that he had committed.[6] This is the type of resignation which can accompany the preliminary procedure of the administrative removal of pastors.[7] In such cases the grave fear, if present, is certainly justly inspired in the incumbent.

By means of its specific and clear legislation with reference to the effect that fear has upon a renunciation of office, the Code has settled all the doubts that existed in the law prior to the year 1918. In the present law a resignation is definitely invalid if it is effected by means of grave and unjustly inspired fear.

Article II. Freedom from Deceit and Error

Deceit and error are two elements which are closely related one to the other. Although error may arise from various sources, it is often caused by deceit. In the matter of a renunciation of office, however, the effects produced by deceit and error are different. For this reason it is necessary to treat these two elements separately.

Section 1. Freedom from Deceit

Labeo (50? B. C.–18 A. D.) defined deceit as follows: "*Omnis calliditas, fallacia, machinatio ad circumveniendum, fallendum, decipiendum alterum adhibita.*" [8]

Deceit is substantial or accidental according to whether it gives rise to substantial or accidental error. The deceit may be

[6] *Caietana,* 24 apr. 1880—*Fontes,* n. 4246.

[7] Can. 2148, § 1; 2158.

[8] D. (4, 3) 1.

causative, that is, the person is induced by it to place his act, or it may be simply concomitant, that is the person is not induced by it to place his act inasmuch as he would nevertheless have placed the same act even if he had known that deceit was being employed.

Canon 103, § 2, states that acts placed under the influence of deceit are valid unless the law decrees otherwise. They may be rescinded, however, in the same way as acts which are placed under the influence of an unjustly inspired grave fear. If the deceit is the cause of substantial error, then any act placed under such a condition is invalid, since substantial error renders all acts null.[9]

Canon 185, in treating of deceit with reference to the act of renunciation of office, declares that deceit renders the resignation invalid. There is a difference of opinion among the authors with reference to the interpretation of the canon on this point. In order the better to understand the reason for this difference, it seems advisable to quote the canon here. It reads as follows:

> *Renuntiatio ex metu gravi, iniuste incusso, dolo aut errore substantiali vel simoniace facta, irrita est ipso iure.*

Some authors maintain that the word "*substantiali*" modifies both "*dolo*" and "*errore,*" and therefore they contend that only substantial deceit renders a resignation invalid.[10] Others consider that this canon is an exception to the general rule contained in canon 103, § 2, and hold that accidental deceit also renders a resignation invalid.[11] In other words, the latter authors consider the word "*substantiali*" as modifying only the noun "*errore.*"

The writer believes that the latter interpretation is favored by the very construction of the canon. Besides, the legislator mani-

---

[9] Can. 104.

[10] Vermeersch-Creusen, *Epitome,* I, n. 304; Maroto, *Institutiones,* I, n. 680; Wernz-Vidal, *Ius Canonicum,* II, n. 328.

[11] Coronata, *Institutiones,* I, n. 263; Blat, *Commentarium,* I, n. 132; Cocchi, *Commentarium,* II, n. 10; Claeys Bouuaert-Simenon, *Manuale,* I, n. 257; J. Salsmans, "Circa vitia consensus"—*Jus Pontificium* (Romae, 1921–), X (1930), 106–107.

fests in the Code a tendency to grant greater protection to acts placed in consequence of deceit than to acts placed through error arising from a source other than deceit. In canon 103, § 2, the legislator provides for the rescission of any act placed in consequence of accidental deceit, while no such provision is made for acts placed through accidental error. Canon 104 provides for the rescission of acts placed through accidental error only in the case of contracts, and this provision is further limited by the prescription of canon 1684, § 2, which permits such rescissory action only for a period of two years and only when the person has suffered a loss greater than half of what the contract stipulated. Since this tendency is apparent in the Code, and since the word "*substantiali*" is not clearly related to the word "*dolo*," the writer prefers to follow the opinion which holds that even accidental deceit invalidates a renunciation of office.

Thus any deceit, substantial or accidental, by which a person is induced to renounce an office, or by which a superior is induced to accept the resignation, renders the resignation invalid. A false representation of the financial condition of a parish, for example, could induce the pastor to resign, or likewise could cause the superior to accept a resignation which he would not otherwise accept. In either case the resignation would be invalid. If the deceit is only accidental, then, of course, it must be the cause of the resignation or of the acceptance of it. If these acts would have been placed in spite of the deceit, then the accidental deceit would not invalidate them.[12]

SECTION 2. FREEDOM FROM ERROR

In the preceding discussion on deceit much has already been said with reference to error and its effects upon acts in general. For this reason the remarks on error will be brief.

Error is a false judgment concerning an object. It may be substantial or only accidental. The former touches the very essence of the thing under consideration, while the latter extends only to accidental qualities of it.

[12] Cf. Gillet, "De actione rescissoria ob dolum"—*Jus Pontificium,* IX (1929), 323–324; Roberti, "De actione rescissoria ob dolum"—*Apollinaris* (Romae, 1928–), III (1930), 143–144.

Substantial error, as also error concerning an accidental quality, which is made a *sine qua non* condition of consent, renders an act invalid.[13] In the latter type of error true consent is also lacking, for, although the error is objectively accidental, it is subjectively substantial.[14]

Canon 185 in conformity with the general rule in canon 104 declares that substantial error invalidates a renunciation of office. If the error is merely accidental, the resignation is valid and not rescissible, since rescissory action is permitted for accidental error only in the matter of contracts.[15] If, however, the accidental error is caused by the use of deceit, then, according to the rules already given with reference to deceit, the resignation is invalid, for accidental deceit renders a resignation invalid.

Article III. Freedom from Simony

The Church has ever been watchful to keep all ecclesiastical offices free from the stain of simony, the crime which has done and can do so much harm to the Church in her work for the salvation of souls. In keeping with this policy, the Church has provided legislation to insure the renunciation of an ecclesiastical office against the evils of this crime. Thus the Code declares that a renunciation of office is invalid if it is made simoniacally.[16] In order properly to understand the meaning of this canon, it is necessary to give a brief summary of the concept of simony as found in the Code.

Simony as forbidden by the divine law is the deliberate design of buying or selling for a temporal price things which are spiritual in themselves or which are annexed to spiritual things; or of making the spiritual thing at least a partial object of the contract.[17] The temporal price involved may be either: (a) *munus a manu,* which is constituted by money or something that

[13] Can. 104.

[14] Coronata, *Institutiones,* I, n. 152.

[15] Can. 104.

[16] Can. 186.

[17] Can. 727, § 1; cf. Ryder, *Simony,* The Catholic University of America Canon Law Studies, n. 65 (Washington, D. C.: The Catholic University of America, 1931), p. 52. The definitions and divisions are taken from this work.

can be reckoned in terms of money; (b) *munus a lingua,* which consists of oral commendation, public expression of approval and the like; (c) *munus ab obsequio,* which involves service of any kind not due by reason of a mutual obligation, but rendered with a view to obtaining a spiritual favor.[18]

Simony as proscribed by the ecclesiastical law consists in the exchange of a spiritual thing for another spiritual thing, or of temporal objects annexed to spiritual things for other temporal objects of the same quality, or even of temporal objects for other temporal objects then, namely, when such an exchange is forbidden by the Church because of the danger of irreverence to spiritual things.[19]

Simony of either of these two classes may be either conventional or real. Conventional simony is had when there is a pact either express or tacit between the parties. It is called mixed conventional simony when the pact is partially fulfilled by at least one of the parties. It is called real simony, on the other hand, when the pact is fulfilled at least partially by both parties.

These principles will be applied in the first place to simony with reference to the renunciation of an ecclesiastical office as such. This consideration will be followed by a treatment of simony with reference to the renunciation of an office which is at the same time a benefice.

Canon 185 states that a renunciation of office made simoniacally is by law invalid. How can a renunciation of office be made simoniacally? The Code contains no prohibition with reference to a renunciation of an office as such which can be understood as constituting a kind of simony which runs counter solely to the ecclesiastical law. Hence the only type of simony which may occur in the resignation of an office as such is simony which the divine law proscribes. This is committed by the giving of a temporal price for the renunciation of an office. An ecclesiastical office is a spiritual thing, and hence the renunciation of it must likewise be considered the giving up of something which is spiritual. In many cases the person who pays a temporal price for a resignation would have at the same time the intention of

---

[18] C. 114, C. I, q. 1; cf. Ryder, *op. cit.*, pp. 57–61.

[19] Can. 727, § 2.

procuring the office for himself or for another party, but this incidental factor is not essential for constituting a simoniacal resignation.

If, for example, a person pays a temporal price to the incumbent for resigning his office merely because the person does not relish any personal contact with the incumbent in his business dealings, the writer believes that such a resignation is simoniacal, for it is the giving of a temporal price in consideration of a spiritual thing, namely, an ecclesiastical office now relinquished through the act of resigning it. In the same manner it is simony if a temporal price is paid to the superior in order that he accept a resignation tendered to him by the incumbent of an office. Hence, the simony may be committed by the incumbent, by the accepting superior or by a third party.[20]

In order to avert the danger of simony in the resignation of an office, the Code declares that an ordinary cannot validly confer on his own or the resigning party's household members, or the relatives by affinity or consanguinity up to and including the second degree, any office made vacant by an act of renunciation.[21] If the ordinary should violate this law and confer a resigned office on one of the aforementioned persons, this fact would not mean that the resignation was simoniacal. The conferral of the office would be invalid by reason of the prescriptions of canon 157. In other words, a violation of canon 157 does not constitute a simoniacal resignation proscribed by the ecclesiastical law. Thus, it remains true that there is no simony proscribed by the ecclesiastical law with reference to the resignation of an ecclesiastical office as such.

All that has been said with reference to offices in general applies as well to offices which are at the same time benefices.[22] There are, however, some special prescriptions which apply only to offices which are at the same time benefices. In other words, there are some prescriptions in the Code which constitute simony proscribed by the ecclesiastical law with reference to the renun-

---

[20] Coronata, *Institutiones,* I, n. 263; Maroto, *Institutiones,* I, n. 680.
[21] Can. 157.
[22] Can, 146.

ciation of an ecclesiastical benefice. These prescriptions are contained in canon 1486, which reads as follows:

> *Dimissionem beneficiorum in commodum aliorum vel sub aliqua conditione, quae ipsam beneficii provisionem aut redituum erogationem attingat, Ordinarius admittere nequit, nisi in casu quo beneficium sit litigiosum et dimissio fiat ab alterutro ex litigantibus in commodum alterius.*

This canon reproduces the pre-Code legislation on conditional resignation and confidential simony in the matter of benefices.[23] Under the earlier law a resignation of a benefice was simoniacal and null if any pact or condition intervened without the authority of the Roman Pontiff. Thus a resignation in favor of another party, or with a reservation of the right to return to the benefice at a later date, or with a reservation of a pension was null unless the authority of the Roman Pontiff sanctioned such conditions.[24]

The Code has retained the concept of confidential simony in canon 1486 in its entirety, but it is no longer a special type of simony carrying with it its own penalties. In the Code it has been assimilated to common simony as proscribed by the ecclesiastical law, and as such is subject to the sanctions placed upon conventional and real simony.[25]

Hence, a resignation of a benefice made contrary to the prescriptions of canon 1486 constitutes simony as proscribed by the ecclesiastical law, and the resignation is thereby null in accordance with the prescriptions of canon 185, which declares a simoniacal resignation to be null and void. The Pontifical Com-

---

[23] Cf. Paulus IV, *motu propr.*, "*Inter caeteras,*" 27 nov. 1557—*Fontes,* n. 92; Pius IV, const. "*Romanum Pontificem,*" 17 oct. 1564—*Fontes,* n. 106; Pius V, const. "*Quanta Ecclesia,*" 1 apr. 1568—*Fontes,* n. 125; Pius V, const. "*Intolerabilis,*" 1 iun. 1568—*Fontes,* n. 130; S. C. C., *Terracinen. seu Setina Cappellaniae,* 19 sept. 1789—*Thesaurus Resolutionum,* LVIIII, 208; S. C. C., *Nullius S. Iacobi de Spatha,* 21 apr. 1792—*Fontes,* n. 3878.

[24] Cf. Garcia, *Tractatus de Beneficiis,* pars XI, c. III, n. 145; Pirhing, *Jus Canonicum,* lib. I, tit. IX, n. 85; Reiffenstuel, *Jus Canonicum,* lib. I, tit. IX, n. 80; Wernz, *Ius Decretalium,* II, n. 498.

[25] Ryder, *Simony,* p. 71; Mostaza, "De Simonia confidentiali in Codice Iur. Can., deque requisitis in quovis delicto simoniae ex parte actus ad poenas canonicas contrahendas"—*Periodica,* XX (1931), 118–120.

mission for the Interpretation of the Code has given a response to the effect that the ordinary may accept the resignation of a pastor with the reservation of a pension chargeable to the benefice for the lifetime of the pensioner in favor of the resigning pastor, provided that the pension does not exceed one-third of the net revenue of the benefice.[26] In the light of this response it is evident that a resignation of this type does not constitute a violation of canon 1486, and hence is not in any way simoniacal in character.

Besides effecting the nullity of the renunciation of the office or benefice, simony is also the cause of the contracting of penalties by the delinquents. Those who are guilty of simony with reference to ecclesiastical offices, benefices or dignities incur automatically an excommuncation reserved in a simple manner to the Holy See, and are perpetually deprived of the right of election, presentation or nomination if they possessed such a right. Besides, clerics are to be suspended.[27] All simoniacal transactions concerning offices are contemplated in the canon which enacts this penalty, and among these transactions a simoniacal resignation has its place.[28]

---

[26] 20 maii 1923, ad IX—*AAS,* XVI (1924), 116.

[27] Can. 2392.

[28] Ryder, *op. cit.,* p. 129.

CHAPTER IX

THE FORM, THE ACCEPTANCE, THE REVOCATION AND THE PUBLICATION OF AN EXPRESS RENUNCIATION

ARTICLE I. THE FORM OF AN EXPRESS RENUNCIATION

Can. 186. *Renuntiatio, ut valida sit, fieri debet a renuntiante aut scripto aut oretenus coram duobus testibus aut etiam per procuratorem speciali mandato munitum; et scriptum renuntiationis documentum in Curia deponatur.*

Thus a valid renunciation may be made either personally or through the medium of a procurator who has a special mandate which empowers him to act in this matter; in either case the resignation may be written or oral, but, if it is oral, then it must be expressed in the presence of two witnesses.

Ordinarily a resignation will be tendered personally by the incumbent, and in writing. There is nothing stipulated in the law as to the contents of a letter of resignation, but it is certainly necessary that the letter express clearly the fact that a resignation of a specific office is being tendered. Since a just cause is required in order that one may licitly renounce an office, this cause should also be indicated in the letter. It is not necessary that the letter be written exclusively for the purpose of tendering a resignation. The resignation may form part of a letter which was written primarily for the transaction of some other business. The statement of the resignation must have the signature of the incumbent affixed to it, or at least proof must be available that the incumbent authorized the written statement with the intention of tendering his resignation.

The canon prescribes that a written document of the resignation be placed in the curia. When the resignation is made in writing by the incumbent, then his letter of resignation is the document that should be put on file in the archives. It is to be noted that the requirement of filing a written document of the resignation does not bind under pain of nullity of the resignation. It is merely a measure which seeks to avert any litigation in the future. Hence, any authenticated document which attests the fact of the resignation will satisfy the prescriptions of the canon. Vidal (1867–1938) remarks that although the recording of the resignation was not prescribed in the old law, nevertheless the Roman and episcopal curias had observed such a practice for a long time.[1]

If the resignation is made orally by the incumbent, then, in order that it be valid, it is necessary that he express his intention in the presence of two witnesses. In this case an authentic document should be composed by the chancellor or another notary, and the document should be placed in the archives.[2] There are no special qualifications required in the witnesses of an oral resignation. Ordinarily they will be priests who are employed in the chancery office, since most of the oral resignations will presumably be tendered to the bishop in his office in the chancery. In the majority of cases it may be assumed that the bishop will ask the incumbent to put his intentions in writing.

The rule of law, "*Potest quis per alium quod potest facere per seipsum,*"[3] is applicable to the matter of a renunciation of office. Thus a person may resign through the medium of a proxy. According to canon 186 the procurator must have a special mandate which empowers him in the name of the incumbent to resign the office. As long as the authorization can be proved, the special mandate may be conceded in writing or orally.[4]

The procurator may depute another to act in his place unless this substitution is forbidden to him in the mandate.[5] When a resignation is made through the medium of a procurator, then

---

[1] *Ius Canonicum,* II, n. 328.

[2] Chelodi, *Ius de Personis,* p. 250, footnote 1; Coronata, *Institutiones,* I, n. 263.

[3] Reg. 68, R. J., in VI°.

[4] Connors, *Extra-judicial Procurators in the Code of Canon Law,* The Catholic University of America Canon Law Studies, n. 192 (Washington, D. C.: The Catholic University of America Press, 1944), p. 8.

[5] *Ibid.,* p. 11.

special mention of the mandate should be made at least in the document of resignation which is deposited in the curia.[6] It would be better to insert a copy of the mandate, or even the mandate itself, in the archives along with the document of the resignation.[7] If the mandate is given orally, then an authentic document which attests this fact should be made by the notary and then placed in the archives. Like the incumbent himself the procurator may execute the resignation either in writing or orally before two witnesses. In either case a written document of the resignation in the sense already explained must be deposited in the curia.

The procurator may make use of his power at any time provided that the special mandate has not ceased to have force. This cessation of the mandate may occur in various ways, namely, by the death of the principal, by the death of the procurator, by revocation or renunciation of the mandate, or by expiration of the time fixed for the execution of the mandate.[8]

A special decree issued by Clement V in the Council of Vienne (1311–1312) ruled that a renunciation of any dignity or benefice made through a procurator was valid even though the principal had already revoked the mandate prior to its execution, if at the time of the execution neither the procurator nor the superior knew of the revocation; if, however, the knowledge of the revocation was kept from them by evil design, then the renunciation was not valid.[9] This principle is still applicable after the Code.[10]

For the validity of a renunciation of office, then, the resignation must be tendered either in writing or orally before two witnesses; it must be made either by the incumbent himself or by his procurator possessing a special mandate which was given either in writing or orally. All the other requirements with reference to the filing of the various documents in the curia affect only the licitness of the resignation. It is to be noted that the prescriptions regarding the form of the resignation apply

---

[6] Coronata, *Institutiones,* I, n. 263.

[7] Chelodi, *Ius de Personis,* p. 250, footnote 1.

[8] Connors, *op. cit.,* pp. 12–14.

[9] C. un., *de renuntiatione,* I. 4, in Clem.

[10] Connors, *op. cit.,* p. 14.

also to a resignation which does not require the acceptance of the superior for its validity.

ARTICLE II. THE ACCEPTANCE AND THE REVOCATION OF AN EXPRESS RENUNCIATION

Can. 189, § 2. *Renuntiationem Ordinarius loci intra mensem vel admittat vel reiiciat.*

Can. 190, § 1. *Officium, renuntiatione legitime facta et acceptata, vacat postquam renuntianti significata est acceptatio.*

§ 2. *Renuntians in officio permaneat donec de Superioris acceptatione certum nuntium acceperit.*

Can. 191, § 1. *Semel legitime facta renuntiatione, non datur amplius poenitentiae locus, licet renuntians possit officium ex alio titulo consequi.*

If a resignation does not require the acceptance of the superior in order to be effective, then once it has been presented to the proper superior in the proper manner, there is nothing more to be added. The same thing is not true with reference to a resignation which needs the superior's acceptance. There are various things to be considered in a resignation of this kind.

In order that the matter of a submitted renunciation of office be not kept pending for too long a period of time, the Code stipulates that the local ordinary is to accept or reject a resignation within a month's time.[11] Actually, however, this period of a month may be of little telling importance, since a response has stated that the ordinary may accept a resignation even after a month has elapsed, provided that the incumbent has not withdrawn his resignation in the meanwhile and has not notified the ordinary of this revocation.[12]

Although this freedom is granted to the ordinary, the general rule stands which commands him to accept or reject the resignation within a month. If he fails to do so, the incumbent may have recourse to a higher superior to have the resignation accepted by him.[13] However, the ordinary's refusal to act within a month's time may not be interpreted as a rejection of the resig-

[11] Can. 189, § 2.

[12] P. C. I., 14 iul. 1922, ad III—*AAS,* XIV (1922), 526-527.

[13] Coronata, *Institutiones,* I, n. 264.

nation, since he is certainly permitted to accept it even after the lapse of a month. Provided that the ordinary has not received notification of the revocation of the resignation by the incumbent, he may accept the resignation no matter how much time has elapsed. It is not required that the acceptance or rejection of a resignation by the superior, or the revocation of a resignation by the incumbent, be in writing or orally before two witnesses in order to be effective. However, one of these two methods should be used, so that proof in the external forum can be produced in case there is any dispute about the resignation.

It remains now to determine up to what point of time an incumbent may withdraw his resignation once he has submitted it. If the resignation does not need the acceptance of the superior, it may not be revoked once it has been presented to the proper authority. If, however, it needs the superior's acceptance, then it is somewhat uncertain for what duration of time a revocation may be made. In this regard canon 191, § 1, states:

> *Semel legitime facta renuntiatione, non datur amplius poenitentiae locus, licet renuntians possit officium ex alio titulo consequi.*

The Pontifical Commission stated that this canon is to be interpreted in the sense that a person may revoke his resignation before the superior has accepted it.[14] Hence the incumbent may withdraw his resignation either before or after the month has elapsed, provided that he does so before the superior has accepted it.[15] While the majority of the authors is content with the statement to the effect that one may withdraw his resignation before the superior has accepted it, others go farther and state that one may withdraw his resignation up until the time he has received notification of the superior's acceptance.[16]

---

[14] 14 iul. 1922, ad III—*AAS*, XIV (1922), 526–527.

[15] *Periodica de Re Canonica et Morali utilia praesertim Religiosis et Missionariis* (Bruges, 1905–), XI (1922), 167.

[16] Vermeersch-Creusen, *Epitome*, I, n. 307; Sipos, *Enchiridion*, p. 163; Woywod, *A Practical Commentary on the Code of Canon Law* (7. ed., revised by Callistus Smith, 2 vols., New York: Joseph F. Wagner, 1943), I, 74; Beste, *Introductio in Codicem*, p. 211.

Although the response of the Pontifical Commission makes no mention of the notification of the superior's acceptance as being necessary to preclude the incumbent's right of revoking his resignation, nevertheless it seems warranted to interpret the response in this manner. Canon 191, § 1, seems to sustain the incumbent's right of revoking his act of resignation up to the moment when the office becomes vacant, for the canon states that the one who has resigned may then obtain the office through some other title. But he does not lose the erstwhile title until the notification of the acceptance has been intimated to him by the superior, for it is only then that the office becomes vacant.[17]

If the superior should withdraw his act of acceptance before it has been intimated to the incumbent, the incumbent would retain the office by reason of the former title. Since, then, in determining the period of time after which the incumbent may no longer revoke his resignation, canon 191, § 1, mentions that after the lapse of that period he may obtain the office through some other title, the canon seems to sustain his right of revoking his resignation up until the time when he actually loses the former title to his office. Since the loss of the former title does not occur until he has received the notification of the superior's acceptance of the resignation, the incumbent's right of revoking his resignation extends up to that time. Of course, the letter of revocation must have been mailed to the superior before the latter's notification of acceptance has reached the incumbent.

Since an office does not become vacant until notification of the superior's acceptance of the resignation has been made to the incumbent,[18] the incumbent must remain in his office until he receives a certified notice of the superior's act of acceptance.[19] Canon 190 speaks only of a certified notice, and thus some authors remark that the common law does not demand an authentic and direct notification.[20] Maroto adds that particular law may demand an authentic notice of the superior's acceptance of the

[17] Can. 190, § 1.

[18] Can. 190, § 1.

[19] Can. 190, § 2.

[20] Claeys Bouuaert-Simenon, *Manuale,* I, n. 345; Maroto, *Institutiones,* I, n. 683.

resignation in order to effect the vacancy of the office and to permit the incumbent to abandon it.[21] Coronata is of the opinion that the notification must be an authoritative one, because of the fact that the vacancy of the office depends upon it.[22]

Although one may not demand an authentic and direct notification unless particular law prescribes it, nevertheless the importance of the notification dictates that care should be taken to see that the resigning party receives it. When the notification of the acceptance is given orally to the resigning party, there can be no doubt about his having received it. If, however, the notification is sent through the mail or by means of a messenger, then a method should be employed which will permit verification of the fact of the arrival of the notification at its destination. Unless care is taken in this matter, there is danger that the superior may confer an office before it is actually vacant. Canon 150, § 1, declares that such a conferral is invalid, and that the subsequent vacancy does not rectify the invalid conferral. To avoid inconveniences of this nature, the superior should take proper precautions to guarantee that the notification of acceptance arrives at its destination.

In brief, then, a superior may accept the resignation of an incumbent at any time, provided that the incumbent has not revoked his resignation and also brought notice of the revocation to the superior; on the other hand, an incumbent may revoke his resignation at any time before the superior has accepted the resignation and also brought notice of the acceptance to the incumbent. The office becomes vacant when the incumbent receives a certified notification of the acceptance of the resignation by the superior. If the resignation does not need the acceptance of the superior, then, by analogy, one must say that the office becomes vacant when the incumbent has received notification of the arrival of his resignation. It should be noted here also that if the superior has rejected the resignation and has brought notice to the incumbent of this rejection, then a new resignation on the part of the incumbent is required before a valid resigna-

---

[21] *Loc. cit.*

[22] *Institutiones,* I, p. 305, footnote 6.

tion can ensue. The law makes no provisions in this regard, but by analogy one may apply the same principles which govern the acceptance of the resignation.[23]

ARTICLE III. THE PUBLICATION OF AN EXPRESS RENUNCIATION

Can. 191, § 2. *Acceptata renuntiatio tempestive nota fiat iis qui aliquod ius in officii provisionem habent.*

The complex and severe method of the publication of a resignation as prescribed by Gregory XIII finds no place in the Code.[24] The Code orders that notification of the vacancy of the office should be given in due time to those who enjoy any right in the conferral of the office involved. If no definite time for the conferral of the office has been prescribed, then the conferral is not to be deferred for a period of more than six months of available time.[25] The six months of available time are to be reckoned from the time that those with whom it rests to fill the office have received the notification of the vacancy.[26] Although the time is available time and does not begin to lapse until the notification has been made, the law does not wish that the conferral of offices be unduly delayed, and hence the superior who accepts the resignation should notify as soon as possible the electors, the patron, or any one else who enjoys any right in the conferral of the office.

As has already been seen, the Code also prescribes that a written document of the resignation be deposited in the curia. This point has been explained above in conjunction with the form of a renunciation. These two prescriptions are the only ones in the Code which bear any resemblance to the publication

---

[23] Cf. Wernz-Vidal, *Ius Canonicum,* II, n. 331. Here the author makes a distinction between the "*perfectio*" and the "*peremptio*" of a resignation. The former occurs when the incumbent receives notification of the superior's acceptance of the resignation; the latter when he receives the notification of the rejection of the resignation.

[24] Const. "*Humano vix iudicio,*" 5 ian. 1584—*Fontes,* n. 152.

[25] Can. 155.

[26] Dubé, *The General Principles for the Reckoning of Time in Canon Law,* The Catholic University of America Canon Law Studies, n. 144 (Washington, D. C.: The Catholic University of America Press, 1941), p. 240.

of a resignation as prescribed in the earlier law. In the present law the prescriptions do not bind under pain of nullity of the resignation.

Finally, it may properly be noted here that the prescriptions regarding the publication of a resignation should be observed also in the case of a tacit renunciation. The reasons for the publication are verified in the case of a tacit renunciation as well as in the case of an express renunciation of office.

CHAPTER X

THE CONCEPT OF A TACIT RENUNCIATION

Besides express renunciation of an eccclesiastical office the Code takes cognizance of another type of resignation which it terms a tacit renunciation. This type of resignation obtained in law before the Code, but the term "tacit renunciation" was never expressed in any law. It was used by the authors to designate a type of resignation which was effected by the placing of certain specific acts. Today, the term "tacit renunciation" is used by the Code itself to designate this type of resignation. The legislation of the Code on tacit renunciation is contained in canon 188, which reads as follows:

> *Ob tacitam renuntiationem ab ipso iure admissam quaelibet officia vacant ipso iure et sine ulla declaratione, si clericus:*
>
> 1°. *Professionem religiosam emiserit, salvo, circa beneficia, praescripto can. 584;*
> 2°. *Intra tempus utile iure statutum vel, deficiente iure, ab Ordinario determinatum, de officio provisus illud adire neglexerit;*
> 3°. *Aliud officium ecclesiasticum cum priore incompatibile acceptaverit et eiusdem pacificam possessionem obtinuerit;*
> 4°. *A fide catholica publice defecerit;*
> 5°. *Matrimonium, etiam civile tantum, ut aiunt, contraxerit;*
> 6°. *Contra praescriptum can. 141, § 1 militiae saeculari nomen sponte dederit;*
> 7°. *Habitum ecclesiasticum propria auctoritate sine iusta causa deposuerit, nec illum, ab Ordinario monitus, intra mensem a monitione resumpserit.*
> 8°. *Residentiam, qua tenetur, illegitime deseruerit et receptae Ordinarii monitioni, legitimo impedimento non detentus, intra congruum tempus ab Ordinario praefinitum, nec paruerit nec responderit.*

As the law itself states, the placing of any of the acts mentioned in this canon effects the vacancy of the cleric's office without the need of any declaration on the part of the superior. This effect is attributed to a tacit renunciation as sanctioned by the law itself. It is called a tacit renunciation to distinguish it from an express renunciation which is made according to the various formalities prescribed in the law. In a tacit renunciation no formalities are prescribed. All that is necessary is that the cleric perform one of the acts or be accountable for one of the omissions to which the law attaches the effect of a tacit renunciation of office. In reality a tacit renunciation resembles a privation, but it can not be considered a privation since the law terms it a tacit renunciation. In the old law Wernz preferred to use the expression, "*ablationes ob factum non-criminosum,*" rather than the term "tacit renunciation," because of the fact that this type of vacancy was effected even when the person had no intention of relinquishing his office.[1] This argument can not be used now, since the Code has officially adopted the term "tacit renunciation" to designate this specific way of losing an ecclesiastical office.

When the law states that an office becomes vacant by a tacit renunciation, what is the force of this expression? In other words, what is the true concept of a tacit renunciation? Some authors state that the law presumes a resignation in these instances.[2] Coronata adds that canon 188 furnishes an example of a presumption "*iuris et de iure.*"[3] Such a presumption can be removed only indirectly, that is, by an undermining of the foundation upon which the presumption rests.[4] Toso is not certain that a presumption is involved in a tacit renunciation, but he says that if there is a question of a presumption here, it is a presumption "*iuris et de iure.*"[5]

The writer is of the opinion that there is no presumption in-

---

[1] *Ius Decretalium,* II, n. 531.

[2] Coronata, *Institutiones,* I, n. 260; Maroto, *Institutiones,* I, n. 684; Augustine, *A Commentary,* II, pp. 160–161; Chelodi, *Ius de Personis,* n. 149.

[3] *Loc. cit.*

[4] Can. 1826.

[5] *Commentaria Minora,* II, 154.

volved in the sanction which the law attaches to a tacit renunciation. A presumption is a probable conjecture of an uncertain thing.[6] What is the thing that is being presumed by the law in a tacit renunciation? Certainly the law is not presuming the actual intention of the person to resign when he places these acts, for in many cases it is absolutely certain that the person has the contrary intention of retaining his office when he does these things. The vacancy of the office is effected by the placing of these acts, even if the person should manifest his intention of retaining the office at the time he places the act. The tacit renunciation occurs in spite of any contrary intention on the part of the incumbent. The law does not merely presume a resignation in these cases. Rather, it attaches the effect of a resignation to these acts when placed by the incumbent. And if the incumbent demonstrates that he did not place any of the acts enumerated in canon 188, then he is not simply destroying a presumption, but he rather is certifying the claim that he did not place an act to which the law attaches the effect of a tacit renunciation.

The writer believes that the law accepts the acts enumerated in canon 188 as equivalent in juridical effect to the full formalities prescribed for the execution of an express renunciation. If a person places an express renunciation, one does not say that it is presumed that he has resigned his office. The resignation is a fact and, unless the person can prove that there was something lacking for the validity of the resignation, the resignation is a closed issue. In like manner, if a cleric places one of the acts enumerated in canon 188, his resignation is not presumed by the law, but it is a fact as sanctioned by the law, and unless he can prove that there was some substantial vitiation of the act, the resignation stands. The fact that the law calls it a tacit renunciation, and not a presumed resignation, is another argument in favor of this opinion, for the words have entirely different meanings. Hence, the writer is of the opinion that a tacit renunciation is a true renunciation and not merely a presumed one. It is tacit because it does not observe the formalities

[6] Can. 1825.

required for an express renunciation, but it is equivalent to an express renunciation in all its effects. The law attaches the effect of a resignation to these acts, but it is not presuming a resignation or an intention of resigning.

Even if it were true that no important difference of consequence would follow from considering a tacit renunciation simply in the nature of a presumed resignation, yet the writer believes that it is a mistaken terminology which makes "tacit" and "presumed" equivalent in meaning. The authors before the Code quite commonly employed these two terms interchangeably,[7] but in spite of this fact the writer believes that such a usage is lacking in precision. In concluding this discussion the writer quotes as a more fitting description of a tacit renunciation the one given by Wernz-Vidal:

> *. . . ius in certis factis agnoscit contineri tacitam renuntiationem, quam ipsum ius admittit et sancit tamquam sequelam iuridicam illius facti, quin opus sit ulla declaratione.*[8]

It is to be noted that every type of office becomes vacant by means of a tacit renunciation when the incumbent places one of the acts specified in canon 188, for the canon uses the words "*quaelibet officia.*" Likewise all clerics come under the prescriptions of this canon since the canon makes no distinction. While cardinals are not subject to the penal law unless they are expressly mentioned,[9] the writer believes that they are subject to the prescriptions of canon 188 without any such special mention, since in his opinion this canon is not a penal canon. It is true that some of the acts enumerated in canon 188 constitute delicts, and have special penalties attached to them, but the effect of a tacit renunciation is not to be considered in the nature of a canonical penalty.

In treating of public defection from the faith, Coronata notes that the tacit renunciation which results in consequence of this

---

[7] Schmalzgrueber, *Jus Ecclesiasticum,* lib. I, tit. IX, n. 2; Reiffenstuel, *Jus Canonicum,* lib. I, tit. IX, n. 9; Santi, *Praelectiones,* lib. I, tit. IX, n. 3.

[8] *Ius Canonicum,* II, n. 329.

[9] Can. 2227, § 2.

defection is not strictly the effect of a penal sanction.[10] This statement is quite true. Certainly the tacit renunciation can not be considered a penalty for a religious profession, which according to canon 188, n. 1, effects a tacit renunciation. There is certainly nothing in such an act that would warrant a penalty. Even with regard to the acts in canon 188 which constitute crimes the writer believes that the tacit renunciation is not inflicted as a penalty. This fact seems quite clear to the writer, especially in view of the manner in which the Code refers to the tacit renunciation in the canons which treat of penalties. The quotation from the following two canons will serve to demonstrate the distinction that the Code makes. Canon 2168, § 2, in treating of the procedure against non-resident clerics, states the following:

> *In monitione Ordinarius recolat* poenas *quas incurrunt clerici non residentes* itemque praescriptum can. 188, n. 8. . . .

Canon 2314, in dealing with the crime of those who are guilty of heresy or apostasy, reads as follows:

> § 1, 3. *Si sectae acatholicae nomen dederint vel publice adhaeserint, ipso facto infames sunt et,* firmo praescripto can. 188, n. 4, clerici, monitione incassum praemissa, degradentur.

The same procedure is followed in the other canons which make mention of a tacit renunciation. It is plainly evident that a distinction is being made between the threatened or enacted penalty on the one hand, and the tacit renunciation on the other. Nowhere in the Code is the tacit renunciation called a penalty. It is always set off in a separate ablative absolute clause when it is enumerated with penalties. For this reason the writer is of the opinion that a tacit renunciation is not to be classified as a penalty. The authors do not expressly designate it as a penalty, but they do list it along with the penalties when they consider the juridic effects consequent upon specific crimes.[11]

---

[10] *Institutiones,* IV, n. 1864.

[11] Vermeersch-Creusen, *Epitome,* III, 513; Coronata, *Institutiones,* IV, nn. 2178, 2196.

The direct purpose of this discussion was to demonstrate that cardinals are subject to the prescriptions of canon 188. Concomitantly the presentation of the arguments served the further purpose of clarifying that in this canon the law is not imposing a penalty, but is rather accepting the specified acts as tantamount to an express renunciation of office. It may here be noted also that a tacit renunciation and a privation of office are very similar, but that the law nevertheless consistently places them in different categories.

The list contained in canon 188 is an exhaustive one. The number of acts which effect a tacit renunciation has been considerably increased in the Code. Formerly there were only four ways in which a tacit renunciation was effected, namely, by the reception of a second incompatible office, by a solemn religious profession, by the contraction of marriage on the part of a minor cleric, and by a voluntary enlistment for military service. To these acts the Code has added four other acts which now entail a tacit renunciation instead of the privation of office sanctioned in the former law. Besides, the Code has extended the effect of a tacit renunciation to any kind or mode of religious profession and also to the attempted contraction of marriage on the part of a major cleric. These points will be discussed in the sections treating of the specific acts enumerated in canon 188. A few general remarks have been made here merely for the purpose of directing attention to the fact that there have been some substantial changes made in the law.

In order to bring the treatment of the individual tacit renunciations within the compass of two chapters, the writer has chosen to employ a correspondingly adapted division of the various acts which are listed in canon 188. Of the two remaining chapters, then, the first will treat of the acts which are non criminal; the second will consider the acts which are criminal, namely, in the specific sense that they have determined penalties attached to them in the Fifth Book of the Code of Canon Law.

CHAPTER XI

TACIT RENUNCIATION OF AN OFFICE IN CONSEQUENCE OF NON-CRIMINAL ACTS

Article I. Religious Profession

Can. 188, n. 1. [*Si clericus*] *Professionem religiosam emiserit, salvo, circa beneficia, praescripto can. 584.*

The first act considered by the Code as effecting a tacit renunciation of an ecclesiastical office is the act of religious profession. Before the Code solemn religious profession in an Order approved by the Church effected a tacit renunciation of the benefice possessed by the candidate.[1] Also perpetual profession in the Congregation of the Missionaries of the Immaculate Heart of Mary caused the tacit renunciation of a residential benefice,[2] but, as Wernz noted,[3] it was not clear whether other types of benefices were affected by such perpetual profession, or whether the response of the Sacred Congregation was applicable to all congregations in which perpetual profession was taken. Such discussion is of purely historical importance now, for the Code makes no distinction between the various types of religious profession. Canon 188, n. 1, states merely that a religious profession causes a tacit renunciation of the offices held by the cleric, and canon 584, in providing special prescriptions with reference to benefices, uses the words, "*qualibet professione religiosa.*" Thus in the present law a religious profession, simple or solemn, temporary or perpetual, is included under the prescriptions of canon 188, n. 1. Since a religious profession is the pronouncement of the three vows of poverty, chastity, and obedience in a religious institute approved by the Church,[4] the

[1] C. 4, *de regularibus et transeuntibus ad religionem,* III, in VI°.

[2] S. C. Ep. et Reg., 25 aug. 1903—*Fontes,* n. 2045.

[3] *Ius Decretalium,* II, p. 270, footnote 5.

[4] Schäfer, *De Religiosis,* n. 263; cf. can. 487.

canon under consideration does not apply to those who join a society in which the three vows are not taken.[5]

It is to be noted that only a valid religious profession effects the tacit renunciation of an office or benefice. Cappello, in discussing various opinions on this point, states that while it is speculatively true that only a valid religious profession effects a tacit renunciation, nevertheless, if a person leaves a religious institute after having made an invalid profession and his benefice has already been conferred upon another, an equitable arrangement should be made in his regard. If on discovery of the invalidity of the profession the invalidity is rectified in accordance with canon 586, then no difficulty will ensue. Likewise, if the new possessor has been in peaceful possession of the benefice for a period of three years from the time that the benefice was apparently vacant under the law, then, even though the profession is invalid, the former incumbent may not lay any claim to the benefice if he should leave the religious institute at that time.[6]

There is little difficulty with reference to the tacit renunciation of an ecclesiastical office as such, for such an office becomes vacant at the very moment that the incumbent makes his religious profession. Ecclesiastical offices, however, which are at the same time benefices, present a more complex problem. Canon 188, n. 1, safeguards the prescriptions of canon 584, which states that the lapse of one year from the time of profession is required to effect the vacancy of a parochial benefice, and the lapse of three years is necessary with reference to other types of benefices. These periods of time are to be computed according to the norms of canon 34, § 3, n. 3. Hence the first day is not counted, and the time expires, one or three years later respectively, with the completion of the day which marks the date on which the profession was made. The reason for the limitation of the period of time to one year in the case of a parochial benefice is undoubtedly because of the care of souls that is in-

---

[5] Cappello, "De beneficio possesso a candidato qui religionem ingreditur"—*Periodica,* XXII (1933), 203–204; cf. can. 673, § 1.

[6] *Ibid.,* p. 206.

volved in such a benefice.[7] Hence the cleric who enters a religious institute remains the titular of the benefice until the respective one or three year period of time has expired. The time is computed from the day of the religious profession, and not from the day of entry into the novitiate.

If, however, the incumbent renounces his benefice, there is no necessity of waiting for the expiration of the periods of time mentioned in canon 584 before the benefice may be conferred upon another cleric. The benefice then becomes vacant through the express renunciation of it. It is possible for such a case to occur, for, while a novice can not validly renounce his benefice during the period of his novitiate,[8] there is nothing in the present law to prevent the renunciation of a benefice before one's entry into religion, or during the period of one's temporary profession when the time requisite for effecting the tacit renunciation has not yet expired.[9]

In the present law the ordinary may confer the benefice immediately upon another in such cases. In the law prior to the Code the bishop could not dispose of the benefice until the profession had been made, even though the cleric had renounced the benefice previously,[10] but this prescription has not been included in the Code. Canon 569, § 1, and canon 581, § 1, in which the renunciation is conditioned on the subsequent act of profession, have reference to goods in the strict sense and not to benefices.[11]

While the candidate may renounce his benefice in the manner described above, he may not renounce it on the condition that

---

[7] Cappello, "De vacatione beneficii post emissam professionem religiosam"—*Periodica*, XXII (1933), 102.

[8] Can. 568.

[9] Cappello, "De vacatione beneficii post emissam professionem religiosam"—*Periodica*, XXII (1933), 104–105; "De beneficio possesso a candidato qui religionem ingreditur"—*Periodica*, XXII (1933), 204–205; Beste, *Introductio in Codicem*, p. 398.

[10] Benedictus XIV, ep. "*Ex quo,*" 14 ian. 1747—*Fontes*, n. 374; Bouix, *Tractatus de iure Regularium* (2 vols., Parisiis, 1857), I, p. 592; Santi, *Praelectiones*, lib. III, tit. XXX, n. 27.

[11] Cappello, "De vacatione beneficii post emissam professionem religiosam"—*Periodica*, XXII (1933), 104–105.

he persevere in the religious life. Such a renunciation would be contrary to the prescriptions of canon 188, n. 1, and canon 584, which predetermines a resultant tacit renunciation after the lapse of definite periods of time. Nor may he renounce his benefice with the reservation of a pension to himself unless an indult of the Holy See is granted to that effect, for canon 1486 forbids such conditional resignations.[12]

Granted, then, that a cleric enters a religious institute and does not renounce his benefice either before his entry or during the period of his profession, he remains the titular of the benefice until the required period of time has elapsed. In the case of a parochial benefice provision must be made for the care of souls in the meantime by the appointment of a parochial vicar.[13] This vicar will receive a fit remuneration for his services, the amount of which will be determined by the ordinary. A recent decision of the Sacred Congregation of the Council, approved and confirmed by Pope Pius XII, stated that a member of a chapter who enters a religious institute has no right to the fruits of his benefice during the period of time required by canon 584 for the vacancy of the benefice to be effected unless he possesses an Apostolic indult permitting him to retain the fruits.[14] The Sacred Congregation of the Council with the consent of the Sacred Congregation for Religious treated this question in a general way, and hence, although the decision was given for a particular case, it may safely be applied to all cases in which an incumbent of a benefice enters a religious institute.

While the candidate does not receive the fruits of his benefice during the time which must elapse before the tacit renunciation will take effect, he still remains the titular of the benefice and therefore may resume possession of it if he leaves the religious institute before the expiration of the time at which the tacit renunciation would set in. It must also be remembered that, even if the required time has elapsed for the vacancy of the benefice to set in, or if the cleric has renounced the benefice, the

---

[12] Cappello, "De beneficio possesso a candidato qui religionem ingreditur" —*Periodica,* XXII (1933), 207.

[13] Coronata, *Institutiones,* I, n. 593; Schäfer, *De Religiosis,* n. 267.

[14] 13, 19 apr. 1940—*AAS,* XXXII (1940), 374.

proper ordinary must receive and provide for a cleric in major orders who leaves a religious institute without taking perpetual vows.[15]

Article II. Failure to Take Possession of an Ecclesiastical Office within the Appointed Time

Can. 188, n. 2. [*Si clericus*] *Intra tempus utile iure statutum vel, deficiente iure, ab Ordinario determinatum, de officio provisus illud adire neglexerit.*

When a cleric is appointed to an ecclesiastical office but fails to take possession of it within the prescribed time, the law attaches to such a failure the effect of a tacit renunciation of that office. Regarding this type of tacit renunciation no legislation was contained in the former law. There was specified an *ipso iure* effected privation of office with reference to a cleric who failed to receive the priesthood within a year after his appointment to a parochial benefice,[16] and also with reference to a bishop-elect who failed to receive episcopal consecration within six months after his nomination to the episcopate.[17] Some authors regarded such a forfeiture of office as effected through a tacit renunciation,[18] but the majority of them did not, for the law spoke rather clearly of a privation.

The common law does not provide a general rule regarding the time within which one must take possession of an office. In the case of a bishop, for example, it does provide a rule. A bishop must take possession of his diocese within four months after the reception of the Apostolic letters unless he is detained by a legitimate impediment.[19] Hence, if a bishop fails to take possession of his see within the prescribed time, he loses the see by a tacit renunciation, unless he was prevented from taking possession by reason of a legitimate impediment. This tacit renunciation must not be confused with the penalties which are

---

15 Can. 641, § 1.

16 Cc. 7, 14, 35, *de electione et electi potestate*, I, 6, in VI°.

17 Conc. Trident., sess. XXIII, *de ref.*, c. 2.

18 Schmalzgrueber, *Jus Ecclesiasticum*, lib. I, tit. IX, n. 2; Reiffenstuel, *Jus Canonicum*, lib. I, tit. IX, n. 9.

19 Can. 333.

imposed upon a bishop-elect who fails to receive episcopal consecration within the time prescribed by the law. Canon 2398 deprives a bishop-elect of the fruits of his benefice if he fails to receive consecration within three months, and it deprives him of the episcopal benefice if he fails to receive his consecration within another three-month period. Thus, even though a bishop may take possession of his diocese within the proper time and thus avoid the tacit renunciation of his benefice, he may be deprived of it by his failure to receive the episcopal consecration within the six-month period; on the other hand, even though he may receive episcopal consecration within the first three months, he may lose his see by a tacit renunciation through his failure to take possession of it within the four-month period. While these provisions are closely connected, they remain distinct and separate. One is a tacit renunciation; the other is a privation. One has reference to the failure to take possession of the office; the other refers to the failure to receive episcopal consecration.

Since there is no time limit set in the Code with reference to the taking of possession of ecclesiastical offices in general, one must look to particular law for information on this point. The Code gives the ordinary the power to define the time within which one must take possession of an office or of a benefice.[20] He may make a standing rule which uniformly affects both offices and benefices in the matter of taking possession of them, or he may define the time limit in each individual case. Simenon remarks that in the diocese of Liège in Belgium one must take possession of a parochial benefice within two months from the day of the appointment.[21] The time in each case is available time, and therefore it does not lapse if the cleric does not know of the specifically fixed time limit or is unable to take possession because of some legitimate impediment.[22] The time is computed according to the norms of canon 34, § 3, n. 3. Hence the first day is not counted, and the fixed period of time elapses only

[20] Can. 188, n. 2; 1442, § 2.

[21] "Renuntiatio Officiorum Ecclesiasticorum"—*Revue Ecclésiastique de Liège* (Liège: H. Dessain, 1908–), XXII (1930–1931), 186, footnote 3.

[22] Can. 188, n. 2; 35.

with the completion of the last day among the number of days which constitute this period.

If a special form of canonical possession is prescribed by custom or law, then this form must be observed in the taking of possession of the office or benefice. Ordinarily no form is prescribed for the taking of possession of offices which are not benefices. In these cases one has done the equivalent of taking canonical possession of the office when one has reported for actively assuming the duties of office.

Article III. The Reception of a Second Incompatible Office

> Can. 188, n. 3. [*Si clericus*] *Aliud officium ecclesiaticum cum priore incompatibile acceptaverit et eiusdem pacificam possessionem obtinuerit.*

The Code defines incompatibility in two instances. It defines as incompatible such offices which can not be fulfilled by the same person at one and the same time.[23] It defines two benefices as mutually incompatible for the same reason, and also for the case in which one of the benefices is in itself sufficient for the decent sustenance of the incumbent.[24] Both of these descriptions are to be understood in a relative import, and therefore need to be applied by the proper superior in each individual case, except for the few cases in which the Code has seen fit to declare the incompatibility of certain specific offices in relation to each other.

The incompatibility may result from the very nature of the offices or from the multiple duties attached to them. Thus, two parishes are incompatible by reason of the law of residence attached to the office of pastor. Coronata notes that if the nature of the offices is determined by ecclesiastical law, then this law may change their nature, and in this way two offices which were formerly incompatible may become compatible in the light of the newly enacted law.[25] Two offices which are by their nature

---

[23] Can. 156, § 2.

[24] Can. 1439, § 2.

[25] *Institutiones,* I, p. 241, footnote 7.

compatible may be rendered incompatible by a declaration of the law to that effect. A good example of this type of incompatibility is found in the law of canon 1439, § 2, where two benefices are declared incompatible if one of them is sufficient to provide a decent sustenance for the incumbent. Such a prohibition is made to avert any avaricious accumulation of benefices.[26] Thus incompatibility of two offices may arise either from the nature of the offices or from a declaration of the law. Usually the obligation of residence which attaches to the offices, the preponderance of the official duties, the necessity of providing well for the care of souls and the like will constitute the reasons why two offices are incompatible and thus can not be possessed by the same person at any one time.

Canon 156, § 1, states that two incompatible offices are not to be conferred upon anyone. This law is not an invalidating law, for canon 188, n. 3, states that a cleric loses his first office by a tacit renunciation when he has received and taken peaceful possession of the second incompatible office. Thus the conferral of the second office is valid, but the cleric is prevented from retaining both of them by the fact that the first one is tacitly renounced when peaceful possession of the second one is had.

The possession of the second office must be a peaceful possession, that is, one that is uncontested.[27] Also, the two offices must have been conferred upon the cleric in title in order to effect the tacit renunciation of the first office.[28] Hence, if one office is possessed in title and the other is had only by reason of provisory administration, as sometimes happens in regard to parishes and dioceses,[29] the tacit renunciation of the first office does not occur. The same thing is true if two offices, otherwise incompatible, are perpetually united as in the case of two episcopal sees or two parishes.[30]

In order, then, that the tacit renunciation of the first office be

[26] Cocchi, *Commentarium,* II, n. 69.

[27] Toso, *Commentaria Minora,* II, 155.

[28] Maroto, *Institutiones,* I, n. 595; Claeys Bouuaert-Simenon, *Manuale,* I, n. 316; Cocchi, *Commentarium,* II, n. 69.

[29] Cf. can. 339, § 5; 472, n. 2.

[30] Cf. can. 339, § 5; 460, § 1; 1420, §§ 2-3.

effected, a cleric must already possess the first office in title and then receive title to and take possession of the second incompatible office. If, after having taken peaceful possession of the second office or benefice, the cleric presumes to retain the first one along with the second one, then the law automatically deprives him of both.[31] Since this penal canon contains the word "*praesumpserit,*" any reduction of imputability excuses a cleric from the penalty.[32] The first office or benefice, however, remains vacant by reason of the tacit renunciation prescribed in canon 188, n. 3.

As has already been stated, the law contained in canon 156, § 1, which forbids the conferral of two incompatible offices upon any one person, is not an invalidating law. The conferral of the second incompatible office is therefore valid. The law, however, in canons 188, n. 3, and 2396 provides effectively against the possibility of a cleric's retention of both incompatible offices. All that has been said with reference to the conferral of such offices must be considered as applicable only when the offices have been conferred by superiors other than the Holy See, for paragraph 3 of canon 156 makes special regulations concerning the conferral of a second incompatible office by the Holy See.

Since there is a variety of opinions as to the proper interpretation of canon 156, § 3, it is necessary for the sake of clarity to reproduce the text of the law here. It reads as follows:

> *Firmo praescripto can. 188, n. 3, concessio alterius officii a Sede Apostolica facta non valet, nisi in supplici libello mentio prioris incompatibilis habeatur, aut clausula derogatoria adiiciatur.*

A list of the various opinions will be given first. Then, along with a criticism of the other opinions, there will be submitted the opinion which the writer believes to be the tenable one.

Maroto,[33] Cocchi,[34] Claeys Bouuaert-Simenon [35] and Sipos [36]

[31] Can. 2396.

[32] Can. 2229, § 2.

[33] *Institutiones,* I, n. 595.

[34] *Commentarium,* II, n. 69.

[35] *Manuale,* I, n. 316.

[36] *Enchiridion,* p. 148.

interpret this paragraph as having reference to the granting of a dispensation to hold two incompatible offices. Thus, they say that unless there is mention of the first incompatible office in the petition for the second one, or unless the rescript from the Holy See contains a derogating clause, the Holy See does not intend to grant a dispensation to hold both offices when it confers a second incompatible office upon a cleric. If the required mention is made in the petition, or if a derogating clause is contained in the rescript, then the cleric may retain both offices.

Coronata [37] and Chelodi [38] make use of a distinction in their interpretation of the law. They state that if mention of the prior incompatible office is made in the petition for the second office, then the conferral of the second incompatible office by the Holy See is valid, but that the tacit renunciation of canon 188, n. 3, takes place when the cleric takes peaceful possession of the second office. On the other hand, if a derogating clause is contained in the rescript from the Holy See, they maintain that not only is the conferral of the second incompatible office valid, but the cleric may also retain both offices. Thus they consider that the derogating clause produces two effects, namely, it makes the conferral of the second office valid, and it grants a dispensation to hold both offices.

Augustine considers this canon as having reference to a dispensation to hold both offices, but his conclusion is not unmistakably clear.[39] He states that even when a papal rescript which is provided with the necessary clause is granted to hold two offices, one must be resigned and vacated if the offices are incompatible.

Blat states that if mention of the prior incompatible office is made in the petition, then the conferral of the second office is valid, but a tacit renunciation occurs by reason of canon 188, n. 3, when peaceful possession of the second office is had; if a derogating clause is present in the rescript, then the clause must be examined to determine its precise meaning. If it merely supplies the petitioner's failure to mention his other office, then

[37] *Institutiones,* I, n. 217.

[38] *Ius de Personis,* n. 135.

[39] *A Commentary,* II, pp. 114–115.

the conferral of the second office is valid, but the tacit renunciation of canon 188, n. 3, still is effective; if the clause derogates also from canon 188, n. 3, then the cleric may retain both offices.[40]

Finally, Vermeersch-Creusen, with whom the writer agrees, explain the canon in this manner:

> *S. Sedes non vult, nisi conscia, alterum officium ei conferre, qui iam unum cum illo incompatibile detinet.* Quare *rescriptum S. Sedis* concedens alterum officium cum priore incompatibile *non valet,* nisi mentio prioris in supplici libello facta fuerit aut clausula derogatoria adiiciatur.
>
> Intentio tamen S. Sedis non est ut utrumque officium retineatur, ideoque, nisi de speciali dispensatione a can. 188 mentio fiat, capta pacifice possessione novi officii, prius ipso iure ex tacita renuntiatione vacat.[41]

The writer believes that this interpretation of canon 156, § 3, is the proper one. In the writer's opinion this paragraph does not treat at all of the question of obtaining a dispensation to hold two incompatible offices. Rather, it treats of the validity of the conferral of a second incompatible office by the Holy See. According to paragraph one of this canon it is forbidden to confer two incompatible offices on a person, but, as has already been seen, the conferral, if made, is valid, and the first office becomes vacant by the taking of peaceful possession of the second one. This is true when the conferral of the second incompatible office is made by a superior other than the Holy See. Paragraph 3 of canon 156 gives a more stringent rule with reference to the conferral of such an office by the Holy See. According to this paragraph of the law when the Holy See confers a second incompatible office upon a cleric, the very conferral of this second office is invalid, unless there is mention of the former office in the petition or unless there is a derogating clause in the rescript of conferral.

Canon 156, § 3, speaks only of the validity of the conferral of the second office, and not of the granting of a dispensation to hold both offices. This is clearly shown by the fact that the

---

40 *Commentarium,* II, n. 98.

41 *Epitome,* I, n. 274.

entire paragraph comes under the limitation of its opening words, "*Firmo praescripto can. 188, n. 3,*" which demands the tacit renunciation of the first office when the cleric has taken peaceful possession of the second one. The writer does not mean to say that the Holy See can not dispense the cleric in such a way that he may hold both offices. Certainly the Holy See can grant such a dispensation, but that point is not under discussion in canon 156, § 3, for the opening words of the canon expressly state that the prescriptions of canon 188, n. 3, are safeguarded. Hence, if there is mention of the former incompatible office in the petition for the second one, or if there is a derogating clause in the rescript of conferral of the second office, the conferral of the second office is valid, but the cleric loses the first office by a tacit renunciation when he takes peaceful possession of the second one. That, in the writer's opinion, is the proper interpretation of canon 156, § 3.

An examination of the opinions of the other authors will help to substantiate this interpretation.

According to the first group of authors a mention of the other incompatible office in the petition, or a derogating clause in the rescript, not only makes the conferral of the second office valid, but also grants a dispensation to hold both incompatible offices. If this interpretation is accepted, then the words, "*Firmo praescripto can. 188, n. 3*" lose all meaning in canon 156, § 3. If no mention of the other office is made in the petition, or if no derogating clause is present in the rescript, then the conferral of the second office is invalid, and canon 188, n. 3, will remain without applicable effect. If mention is made in the petition, or a derogating clause is present in the rescript, then, since according to these authors a dispensation to hold both offices is granted in such a case, once more canon 188, n. 3, remains inapplicable. In other words, canon 156, § 3, invokes for the prescriptions of canon 188, n. 3, a safeguard which never can come to the point of being realized.

The second opinion advanced by the authors holds that while mention of the other office in the petition merely makes the conferral of the second office valid, a derogating clause in the rescript not only makes the conferral of the second office valid, but also grants a dispensation for the recipient to hold both incompatible offices. The writer fails to see how the text of the law warrants such an interpretation. Once more the writer wishes to assert that he freely grants that the derogating clause may grant a dispensation to hold both offices, but it would have to contain a special mention of canon 188, 3°. Canon 156, § 3, states that the conferral of a second incompatible office by the Holy See is invalid unless there is mention of the other incompatible office in the petition or a derogating clause in the rescript. These two conditions are introduced by the same conjunction, "*nisi*," and are conditions which, if at least one is verified, make valid the conferral of the second office which would otherwise be invalid. The words, "*Firmo praescripto can. 188, n. 3*," constitute a limitation which extends to the whole paragraph of the canon, but they remain unaffected by the *nisi* clauses, for these bear an exclusive relation to the main clause in which by way of a general statement in law the conferral of the second incompatible office by the Holy See is declared invalid.

Augustine's remarks on this canon are quite confusing. He seems to forget that this canon is speaking only of the conferral of incompatible offices. No special dispensation is required for the retention of two compatible offices, nor is there any question concerning the validity of the conferral of such offices.

The only objection that the writer wishes to make against Blat's opinion is the fact that he considers the derogating clause in canon 156, § 3, under a double aspect. He states that the clause in the rescript must be examined to determine whether it proposes merely to supply the petitioner's failure to mention his other office, and therefore intends merely to make the conferral of the second office valid; or whether it has the further purpose of dispensing from the prescriptions of canon 188, n. 3. Materially taken this statement is true, but the writer insists that the derogating clause mentioned in canon 156, § 3, must be regarded not as being primarily concerned with any possible dispensation to hold both offices, but simply with the factors of validity for the conferral of the second office.

Thus the writer believes that when the Holy See confers a second incompatible office on a cleric, the conferral of it is invalid unless mention of the other incompatible offices is made in the petition, or unless a derogating clause is contained in the rescript of conferral. If the required mention is made in the petition, or if a derogating clause is present in the rescript, then the conferral of the second incompatible office is valid, but the first office becomes vacant by a tacit renunciation as soon as the cleric takes peaceful possession of the second incompatible office. A special dispensation from the prescriptions of canon 188, n. 3, is necessary before the recipient of the rescript can validly as well as lawfully continue to hold his earlier office. The Holy See is the only authority which in its own right is competent to grant such a dispensation.

Article IV. Voluntary Military Service

Can. 188, n. 6. [*Si clericus*] *Contra praescriptum can. 141, § 1, militiae saeculari nomen sponte dederit.*

All clerics are by reason of the privilege of clerical immunity free from the obligation of military service.[42] The possession of this privilege is founded upon the very fundamental consideration that the best interests of the clerical and the military state can not be served simultaneously by one and the same individual. There is no violation of distributive justice in the exemption which the privilege grants since there are many other ways of serving one's country than by the bearing of arms.[43] This privilege is a commonly (*communiter*) personal privilege, that is, it is given to a physical person because of the fact that he belongs to a certain state of life. It is also a common privilege, namely, one that is conceded for the common good and not directly for the good of the individual who enjoys it.[44] For these reasons this privilege may not be renounced by the individual cleric acting upon his own authority.[45]

---

[42] Can. 121.

[43] Chelodi, *Ius de Personis*, p. 195, footnote 3; cf. Pius IX, *Syllabus errorum*, prop. 32—*Fontes*, n. 543.

[44] Roelker, *Principles of Privilege according to the Code of Canon Law*, The Catholic University of America Canon Law Studies, n. 35 (Washington, D. C.: The Catholic University of America, 1926), pp. 31–32; 36–37.

[45] Cans. 72; 123; cf. Roelker, *op. cit.*, pp. 108–112.

Besides the general norms which forbid the renunciation of all clerical privileges, the Code makes some special norms with reference to the privilege of immunity from military service. It forbids a cleric to volunteer for military service unless he does so with the permission of the ordinary for the purpose of being more quickly freed of the pending obligation.[46]

The exceptional case in which canon 141, § 1, permits a cleric to volunteer for military service would be verified in a country which, in violation of the privilege of immunity, obliges clerics to perform military service. Thus if a law obliging clerics to military service was passed in a given country, a cleric in that country could volunteer for military service with the permission of the ordinary and in this way free himself from the obligation so that he may continue his studies for the priesthood undisturbed in the future. But in this country there can not arise in the present either any need or any opportuneness which would call for a cleric's enlistment in the military service with the permission of his ordinary inasmuch as all clerics are exempted from military service, not indeed by constitutional law, but simply by an act of congress.[47]

It is to be noted that two things are postulated in canon 141, § 1, if it is to become lawful for a cleric to volunteer for military service, namely, the permission of the ordinary and the purpose of being more quickly freed from the pending obligation. If either of these conditions is lacking, the enlistment entails a violation of the canon, and accordingly subjects the cleric to the effects which the law attaches to such a violation. The effect which is under consideration here is enacted in canon 188, n. 6, which states that a violation of canon 141, § 1, effects the tacit renunciation of any ecclesiastical office the cleric possesses. If the offender is a minor cleric, he falls automatically from the clerical state by such a violation.[48]

The general principles involved in these canons are quite clear, but in order to apply them in practice, it is necessary to determine the meaning of the term "military service." It is not an

[46] Can. 141, § 1.

[47] *The Jurist,* III (1943), 633.

[48] Can. 141, § 2.

easy matter to accomplish, for there has been no official pronouncement on this score, and the authors for the most part do not attempt to offer any fully discriminate explanation.

Coronata maintains that although canons 121, 141, § 1 and 188, n. 6, are directed against a cleric's military service especially in the sense of bearing arms, nevertheless they also apply to the enlistment of a cleric in all other types of military service.[49] Claeys Bouuaert-Simenon, on the other hand, interpret the term "military service" in the cited canons as having reference only to the bearing of arms.[50] Military service in the wide sense of the term, that is, work in the chaplains' corps, in the medical corps, and the like, in their opinion is not interdicted in the prescriptions of these canons. The work involved in these types of service is not strictly alien to the clerical state; as a matter of fact it is often in full accord with it. They admit that the rights of the Church would be violated if the State on its sole authority imposed such obligations on clerics contrary to the wishes of the bishops or without having consulted them on the subject, but they do not consider such action on the part of the State as a violation of the immunity from military service sanctioned in canon 121. Accordingly they contend that a cleric has not violated canon 141, § 1, when he has volunteered for military service in the wide sense of the term. Downs states that the service which is given in the chaplains' corps and the medical corps is not military service in the strict sense of the term, but he does not state clearly whether only military service in the strict sense is intended in canon 121.[51]

Vermeersch-Creusen seem to imply that the military service which is mentioned in the cited canons must be regarded as military service in the strict sense.[52] Commenting on canon 141, § 1, these authors state that a cleric who is obliged to serve in

---

49 *Institutiones,* I, n. 184; *Ius Publicum Ecclesiasticum* (Taurini: Marietti, 1934), n. 154.

50 *Manuale,* I, nn. 279; 301.

51 *The Concept of Clerical Immunity,* The Catholic University of America Canon Law Studies, n. 126 (Washington, D. C.: The Catholic University of America Press, 1941), p. 44.

52 *Epitome,* I, n. 259.

the hospital corps or in an administrative position violates this canon if he transfers to the service of bearing arms. This distinction could not be made by them unless they understood this canon as referring only to military service in the strict sense. If they conceived of this canon as pointing to all types of military service, then the cleric, by making such a transfer, would not be volunteering for military service, since he has already been obliged to give military service in at least the wide sense of the term. The question still remains a very doubtful one. Until some decision has been given in the matter, the writer prefers to follow the opinion that only military service in the strict sense is interdicted in these various canons. Thus only the occupation of a soldier in the capacity of a soldier, namely, that which is directed to actual combat, is considered as military service. Only that type is truly repugnant to the clerical state.

The military service must be performed in an organization which has for its purpose the waging of war in the name of the country to which it pertains. Thus, for all practical purposes, the organization must be the armed forces of a country, as, for example, the army or the navy. Only military service in such an organization constitutes true military service according to the common acceptance of the term.

A question might be raised concerning the National Guards which exist in the various states of the United States. The writer is of the opinion that enlistment in this organization would not constitute a violation of canon 141, § 1, and hence would not cause the tacit renunciation of one's office. The National Guards constitute rather a supplementary police force, whose purpose it is to aid in the maintenance of order in their respective states. It is true that they may be incorporated into the regular army by order of the President of the United States in time of war, but in themselves they are not part of the army, nor are they troops of war, for the Constitution of the United States expressly forbids the individual states to maintain troops of war in times of peace.[53] In a country in which clerics are exempt from military service even in time of war, one would

[53] Art. I, sec. X, par. 3.

certainly jeopardize his status by placing himself in an organization which in all likelihood would be incorporated into the armed forces in the event of war, but the writer does not believe that this possibility or even probability of incorporation would brand his enlistment in the National Guards as a violation of canon 141, § 1.

The same conclusion may be drawn with reference to all other types of organizations of a military nature. Unless the organization is the official military instrument of the perfect society, voluntary enlistment in such an organization would not imply a violation of the law of canon 141, § 1.

Summarizing all that has been said, the writer believes that before he violates the law of canon 141, § 1, and occasions the tacit renunciation of his office as mentioned in canon 188, n. 6, a cleric must have volunteered for military service in the strict sense of the term, that is, for the service which is directly ordered to actual combat and which is performed in an organization which is the official means of defense for the State. Even if a cleric volunteered for such a service, no violation would be had in the event that the cleric enlisted with the permission of his ordinary for the purpose of being more quickly freed from the pending obligation, for canon 141, § 1, permits such an enlistment. Voluntary enlistment for any other type of military service would not constitute a violation of canon 141, § 1, although the cleric could be punished by the ordinary for deserting his charge or for doing things foreign to the clerical state.[54]

---

[54] Cans. 128; 2399; 139, § 1.

CHAPTER XII

TACIT RENUNCIATION OF AN OFFICE IN CONSEQUENCE OF CRIMINAL ACTS

Article I. Public Defection from the Faith

Can. 188, n. 4. [*Si clericus*] *A fide catholica publice defecerit.*

Since it is not only incongruous that one who has publicly defected from the faith should remain in an ecclesiastical office, but since such a condition might also be the source of serious spiritual harm when the care of souls is concerned, the Code prescribes that a cleric tacitly renounces his office by public defection from the faith. Prior to the Code the law imposed a privation of office and benefice on a cleric for such a crime.[1] This penalty was certainly imposed upon those clerics who were publicly guilty of heresy and of apostasy, but because of two apparently contradictory laws it was disputed whether the penalty applied also to those who were publicly guilty of schism.[2] The present law attaches a tacit renunciation instead of a privation of office to a public defection from the faith. Since canon 188, n. 4, uses a general terminology, it is necessary to determine the meaning of a defection from the faith and also to determine the extent of publicity that is required if the act of defection is to become the basis for a tacit renunciation of office.

[1] C. 9, X, *de haereticis,* V, 7—Jaffé, n. 15109; Nicholas II, const. "*Noverit universitas,*" 3 mart. 1280—*Bullarium,* IV, 47; c. 12, *de haereticis,* V, 2, in VI°; c. un., *de schismaticis,* V, 3, in VI°—Potthast, n. 24520; c. un., *de schismaticis,* V, 4, in Extravag. com.—Potthast, n. 25324; Paulus IV, const. "*Cum ex apostolatus,*" 27 ian. 1567—*Fontes,* n. 117.

[2] Cf. Wernz, *Ius Decretalium,* II, n. 537; Gennari, *Sulla Privazione del Beneficio Ecclesiastico e sul Processo Criminale dei Chierici* (2. ed., Romae, 1905), pp. 22-23; 30-31; Lega, *De Iudiciis Ecclesiasticis* (4 vols., Vol. III, 1899, Romae), III, nn. 333-334; 434.

Since three specific crimes, namely, heresy, apostasy and schism, will enter into this discussion, it is necessary to give the definitions of them as found in the Code. These definitions are contained in canon 1325, § 2, which reads as follows:

> *Post receptum baptismum si quis, nomen retinens christianum, pertinaciter aliquam ex veritatibus fide divina et catholica credendis denegat aut de ea dubitat, haereticus; si a fide christiana totaliter recedit, apostata; si denique subesse renuit Summo Pontifici aut cum membris Ecclesiae ei subiectis communicare recusat, schismaticus est.*

These definitions are quite clear. Apostasy is a total defection from the faith, while heresy is only a partial defection, but as MacKenzie remarks,[3] they are essentially the same, since the rejection of any one truth involves the same blasphemous attitude towards God that is involved in a denial of all the truths. Schism, on the other hand, is rather an offense against obedience and charity than against faith, although heresy is almost always joined to it.[4]

The authors are not in agreement as to whether schism is to be included in the meaning of the term "defection from the faith," as used in canon 188, n. 4. Augustine,[5] Blat,[6] Toso[7] and Coronata[8] do not regard schism as constituting a defection from the faith as understood in canon 188, n. 4, since schism as such does not essentially militate against the possible retention of the faith even in its entirety. Maroto,[9] Vermeersch-Creusen,[10] Cocchi[11] and Sipos,[12] on the other hand, consider schism pure

[3] *The Delict of Heresy in Its Commission, Penalization, Absolution,* The Catholic University of America Canon Law Studies, n. 77 (Washington, D. C.: The Catholic University of America, 1932), p. 19.

[4] *Ibid.,* pp. 16–17.

[5] *A Commentary,* II, 161.

[6] *Commentarium,* II, n. 135.

[7] *Commentaria Minora,* II, 155.

[8] *Institutiones,* I, n. 263.

[9] *Institutiones,* I, n. 684.

[10] *Epitome,* I, n. 306.

[11] *Commentarium,* II, n. 101.

[12] *Enchiridion,* p. 164.

and simple as sufficient to constitute a defection from the faith and hence to call for the application of the sanction enacted in canon 188, n. 4. Heneghan includes those who are guilty purely of schism in his interpretation of the clause, "*qui notorie aut catholicam fidem abjecerunt,*" in canon 1065, § 1.[13] The expression which Heneghan interprets in this manner is substantially the same as the expression employed in canon 188, n. 4, which reads as follows: "*A fide catholica publice defecerit.*"

According to the strict interpretation of the words contained in canon 188, n. 4, and of the definition of schism, it must be admitted that the canon does not indisputably comprehend the condition of pure schism, since in its essence schism does not denote defection from the faith, but rather connotes a violation of obedience and charity. However, one could doubt that the law intends to exclude the consideration of schism from this canon, for in canon 2314, § 1, n. 3, which provides penalties for the public adherence to a non-catholic sect, cognizance is taken of canon 188, n. 4, with the words "*firmo praescripto can. 188, n. 4.*" Since the wording of canon 2314, § 1, n. 3, applies to a schismatical sect as well as to a heretical one, and since the application of canon 188, n. 4, is confirmed in this canon, one could reasonably be led to conclude that the wording of canon 188, n. 4, means to comprise also the condition of pure schism.

In practice it will be extremely rare that a case of pure schism will arise, for almost invariably and all but inevitably some heresy will be joined to it. This is especially true since the time of the solemn definition of the primacy and the infallibility of the Roman Pontiff. If, however, there should arise a case of pure schism on the part of a cleric, the writer believes that the cleric would not lose his office by a tacit renunciation since the sanction of canon 188, n. 4, is of but doubtful efficacy in view of its questionable comprehension of the condition of pure schism, and especially since the effective application of that sanction involves the forfeiture of a vested right.[14]

---

[13] *The Marriage of Unworthy Catholics, Canons 1065 and 1066,* The Catholic University of America Canon Law Studies, n. 188 (Washington, D. C.: The Catholic University of America Press, 1944), pp. 96–97.

[14] Cf. can. 19.

The defection from the faith must be public. It is to be noted immediately that adherence to or inscription in a non-catholic sect is not required to constitute the publicity that the canon demands. The defection must be public according to the definition of publicity which is found in canon 2197, n. 1:

> *Delictum est publicum, si iam divulgatum est aut talibus contigit aut versatur in adiunctis ut prudenter iudicari possit et debeat facile divulgatum iri.*

The authors are in agreement that this is the type of publicity postulated for making the defection a public one.[15] Thus the defection from the faith may be public by reason of the fact that it is already known to a notable part of the community. The law does not prescribe any special number as being necessary to constitute a notable part of the community. Determination of this point is left to man's prudent judgment. Besides being public by reason of actual divulgation, the defection from the faith may be public also because of the fact that the circumstances force one to conclude that it will be easily divulged in the future. Thus if even only a few loquacious persons witnessed the defection from the faith, or if the sole and only witness was a taciturn person who later threatened to divulge the crime because of an enmity that has arisen between him and the delinquent, the delict would be public in the sense of canon 2197, n. 1.[16]

A cleric, then, if he is to occasion the tacit renunciation of his office, must have defected from the faith by apostasy or heresy in a public manner according to the explanation just given. Since the writer holds the opinion that a tacit renunciation is not of the nature of a penalty, he holds also that the prescriptions of canon 2229 concerning excusing causes with reference to *latae sententiae* penalties do not apply to the case of a tacit renunciation of office on the part of a cleric who has perpetrated the act which is mentioned in canon 188, n. 4. Thus the writer believes that even if it were thinkable that a cleric was excused

[15] Blat, *Commentarium,* II, n. 135; Cocchi, *Commentarium,* II, n. 101; Coronata, *Institutiones,* I, p. 301, footnote 7; Beste, *Introductio in Codicem,* p. 210.

[16] Cf. Michiels, *De Delictis et Poenis* (Vol. I, Lublin: Universitas Catholica, 1934), I, 117–118; Coronata, *Institutiones,* IV, n. 1645.

from incurring the excommunication involved in a defection from the faith in view of the prescriptions of canon 2229, § 3, n. 1, he still would lose his office by a tacit renunciation. In this regard a tacit renunciation is like an irregularity, which, while in many respects it looks like a penalty, is nevertheless not a penalty in a truly canonical sense.

Article II. Marriage or Attempted Marriage

Canon 188, n. 5. [*Si clericus*] *Matrimonium etiam civile tantum, ut aiunt, contraxerit.*

Before the present Code of Canon Law the marriage of a minor cleric caused the tacit renunciation of any office that he possessed at the time. The Code in the present canon has extended this effect to the marriage of any cleric, major or minor. The law makes no distinction, but merely states that the marriage of a cleric effects the tacit renunciation of his office. The fact that major clerics are now included under this law is further manifested by the mention of canon 188, n. 5, in canon 2388, § 1, which is the penal canon for clerics in major orders who attempt to contract even a so-called civil marriage.

According to the present law of the Code a minor cleric may validly and licitly contract marriage [17] while a major cleric can not do so either validly or licitly.[18] If, however, a minor cleric contracts marriage, he falls automatically from the clerical state unless the marriage is invalid because of force or fear inflicted upon him.[19] No attempt will be made here to determine the interpretation of canon 132, § 2, which prescribes an automatic lapse from the clerical state for a minor cleric who contracts marriage. It is sufficient to say that if a cleric falls from the clerical state, he automatically loses any office that he possesses, for in the present law an office in the strict sense partakes of some power of orders or of jurisdiction,[20] and only clerics can possess such power.[21]

[17] Can. 132, § 2.
[18] Cans. 132, § 1; 1072.
[19] Can. 132, § 2.
[20] Can. 145, § 1.
[21] Can. 118.

In the present discussion the writer restricts himself to the determination of the elements required in a marriage or in an attempted marriage to effect the tacit renunciation of an office as prescribed in canon 188, n. 5, in abstraction entirely from the question of whether or not these elements are sufficient to cause the lapse from the clerical state as prescribed for minor clerics in canon 132, § 2. In some instances the elements may be sufficient to cause both effects; in other instances they may be sufficient to cause the lapse from the clerical state, but insufficient to cause the tacit renunciation of an office. In this latter case the cleric will of course lose his office, not however by a tacit renunciation, but indirectly through the fact that he has fallen from the clerical state. In this discussion the effect of a tacit renunciation alone will be considered.

If a minor cleric contracts a valid marriage, he certainly loses his office by a tacit renunciation. Such a case presents no difficulty. The problem becomes more complex, however, when either a minor or a major cleric contracts a marriage that is invalid. It is certain that a tacit renunciation may be effected by an invalid marriage, for the canon states that a tacit renunciation occurs if the cleric contracts a so-called civil marriage, and such a marriage is always invalid.[22] Besides, it has already been shown that major clerics are included under the sanction of canon 188, n. 5. Yet major clerics can not contract a valid marriage since their sacred orders form a diriment impediment.[23] Does it follow, then, that every invalid or null marriage of a cleric effects the tacit renunciation of his office regardless of the cause of the invalidity or nullity of the marital union? That is the question to be answered here. In other words, this discussion will have for its purpose the determination of the elements requisite for the constituting of an attempted marriage.

The opinions of the pre-Code authors are of very little assistance in the solution of this problem. They were concerned only with minor clerics, who could contract a valid marriage, and hence they held opinions that can not be held in the face of the

[22] Can. 188, n. 5.

[23] Can. 1072.

present legislation. The present day authors have little to say on the subject with reference to canon 188, n. 5. The majority of them treats of the question quite thoroughly with relation to canon 2388, § 1, which contains the penalties inflicted on major clerics who presume to contract marriage. It is true that this canon postulates complete malice in the delinquent, and it is true also that the authors are interested primarily in the penalty of excommunication contained in this canon, but independently of these points they discuss the elements requisite for the constituting of an attempted marriage, and their principles and conclusions on this point can be readily applied to the attempted marriage which is mentioned in canon 188, n. 5.

The authors are in agreement on the point that in order to constitute an attempted marriage there must be something more than mere concubinage, even though the concubinage is public or notorious.[24] The observance of the canonical form of marriage is not necessary, for the law states that a so-called civil marriage is sufficient.[25] With reference to the form of marriage, then, a marriage may be attempted either with the observance of the canonical forms prescribed in canons 1094 and 1098, or simply through the use of the form prescribed by the civil law. Besides, an attempted common law marriage is sufficient even in those states which do not recognize such a marriage, since baptized persons remain unaffected by civil laws requiring a form for entrance into marriage.[26]

The fact that there is a diriment impediment present does not prevent a cleric from attempting marriage. This is true with reference to a major cleric even when there exists a diriment

[24] Cappello, *Tractatus Canonico-Moralis de Censuris iuxta Codicem Iuris Canonici* (3. ed., Taurini: Marietti, 1933), n. 355 (Hereafter this work is cited as *De Censuris*); Ayrinhac-Lydon, *Penal Legislation in the New Code of Canon Law* (New York: Benziger Brothers, 1936), n. 362 (Hereafter this work is cited as *Penal Legislation*); Augustine, *A Commentary,* VIII, 475.

[25] Can. 188, n. 5; 2388, § 1; S. C. S. Off. (*Ratisbonen.*), 22 dec. 1880, ad I—*Fontes,* n. 1068.

[26] Dillon, *Common Law Marriage,* The Catholic University of America Canon Law Studies, n. 153 (Washington, D. C.: The Catholic University of America Press, 1942), pp. 127–128.

impediment over and above the impediment of sacred orders.[27] The fact that the individual knows that the marriage is invalid because of the lack of the proper form of marriage or because of the presence of a diriment impediment does not mean that he can not attempt marriage, for the knowledge of the invalidity of the marriage does not necessarily exclude the matrimonial consent.[28] A marriage, then, which is invalid because of the presence of a diriment impediment or because of the non-observance of the canonical form constitutes an attempted marriage.

The problem becomes more difficult with reference to a marriage which is null because of the lack of the proper matrimonial consent. Can such an act be classified as an attempted marriage and therefore effect the tacit renunciation of an office as sanctioned in canon 188, n. 5? There is a divergence of opinion among the authors on this point.

The majority of the authors maintains that if the proper matrimonial consent is not present in both parties either because the consent is merely simulated or because it is vitiated by force, fear or error, then there is no attempted marriage.[29] In other words, these authors demand that there be present the consent which is required to constitute the natural contract of marriage. They all admit that in the external forum the consent is presumed to be present when one goes through any form of marriage, but they maintain that if the consent is not actually present, there is no attempted marriage. Cipollini, on the other hand, while he holds that a simulated consent is not enough to constitute an attempted marriage, maintains that if the matri-

---

[27] S. C. S. Off., 13 ian. 1892—*Fontes*, n. 1147; cf. *Cappello, loc. cit.;* Cipollini, *De Censuris Latae Sententiae iuxta Codicem Iuris Canonici* (2 vols. in 1, Taurini: Marietti, 1925), II, n. 61 (Hereafter this work is cited as *De Censuris*); Cerato, *Censurae Vigentes Ipso Facto a Codice Iuris Canonici Excerptae* (2. ed., Patavii, 1921), n. 64. Hereafter this work is cited as *Censurae Vigentes.*

[28] Cf. can. 1085.

[29] Cappello, *De Censuris*, n. 355; Sole, *De Delictis et Poenis-Praelectiones in Lib. V Codicis Iuris Canonici* (Romae: Pustet, 1920), pp. 385–388; Ayrinhac-Lydon, *Penal Legislation*, n. 362; Cocchi, *Commentarium*, VIII, n. 265.

monial consent is seriously given even though it is a naturally invalid consent, for example, because of substantial error, such a consent constitutes an attempted marriage inasmuch as the cleric has done everything in his power to contract marriage.[30] Cerato goes even farther than Cipollini. He states that there is an attempted marriage even when the consent is simulated.[31] He considers that the validity of the marriage does not receive any consideration, and provided that the external acts are present from which it may be gathered that a marriage has been attempted, that is sufficient to constitute an attempted marriage. He maintains that when the consent is lacking in one party, both parties are culpable, since it is a delict which by its nature demands an accomplice. Vermeersch-Creusen answer this point by saying that in such a case the contract is lacking, and therefore there is no delict.[32]

Smith[33] notes that the opinion which holds that any vitiation of the matrimonial consent of either party to the contract prevents the classification of the act as an attempted marriage has some anomalous consequences. Thus, for example, a cleric would not incur the excommunication [The author is speaking of the excommunication and not of the tacit renunciation, but his remarks are applicable to both effects.] if his partner simulated her consent, and what is worse, he would not incur the excommunication if the consent of the partner was lacking because of violence inflicted upon her by the cleric himself. Such consequences appear strange, but they follow from this opinion.

The writer is inclined to agree with the opinion of Cipollini which states that any serious attempt on the part of the cleric to contract marriage is sufficient to constitute an attempted marriage. Thus, provided that the consent of the cleric is not simulated or vitiated by force or fear, the writer believes that the cleric is guilty of an attempted marriage. This concept of an

---

[30] *De Censuris,* II, n. 61.

[31] *Censurae Vigentes,* n. 64.

[32] *Epitome,* III, n. 592.

[33] *The Penal Law for Religious,* The Catholic University of America Canon Law Studies, n. 98 (Washington, D. C.: The Catholic University of America, 1935), p. 115.

attempted marriage is derived from canon 132, § 2, in which the Code states that a minor cleric falls from the clerical state by marriage unless the marriage is null because of force or fear inflicted upon the cleric. It is true that in things which are *odiosa* one may not make use of analogies, but canon 132, § 2, in the writer's opinion gives an insight into the Code's meaning of an attempted marriage. Common sense prevents the writer from conceding that the legislator wishes to give approval to the almost absurd consequences that follow from the other interpretation of an attempted marriage. However, as Smith remarks,[34] the milder view must be followed until an authentic declaration has been given in the matter. He is speaking primarily of the penalty of excommunication, but his remark applies also to the effect of tacit renunciation, since it, too, is a *res odiosa.*

In practice, then, a cleric loses his office by a tacit renunciation through marriage or even through an attempted marriage, provided that the marriage is not null by reason of a lack of the proper matrimonial consent in either party to the attempt. Since the internal consent is presumed to be in conformity with the signs or words used in the celebration of marriage,[35] the cleric must prove that the consent was lacking in order to escape the tacit renunciation of his office or benefice.

Article III. Failure to Wear the Proper Ecclesiastical Garb

Can. 188, n. 7. [*Si clericus*] *Habitum ecclesiasticum propria auctoritate sine iusta causa deposuerit, nec illum, ab Ordinario monitus, intra mensem a monitione recepta resumpserit.*

The Church has from the earliest times manifested great care in her vigilance over the proper dress of the clergy. The main purpose has been to maintain for the clergy a dress in some way distinct from the ordinary dress of the laity. This effort is clearly shown in the various pieces of legislation enacted throughout the centuries. Some of the legislation prescribed a specific

---

[34] *Loc. cit.*

[35] Can. 1086, § 1.

dress for the clergy while other legislation demanded merely that the dress be distinct from the dress of the laity and proper to the clerical state. The penalty usually invoked against those who violated these laws was a privation of office and benefice. For the sake of a historical background reference is made here to some of the pronouncements made in this regard from the time of the Council of Trent.[36]

The present law on ecclesiastical dress is contained in canon 136, § 1, which reads as follows:

> *Omnes clerici decentem habitum ecclesiasticum, secundum legitimas locorum consuetudines et Ordinarii locorum praescripta, deferant, tonsuram seu coronam clericalem, nisi recepti populorum mores aliter ferant, gestent, et capillorum simplicem cultum adhibeant.*

Since canon 188, n. 7, speaks only of neglect to wear the proper ecclesiastical garb, the discussion will be restricted to this point. It is to be noted that canon 136, § 1, prescribes the dress which is to be worn by clerics in public at a time when they are not performing liturgical functions.[37]

The prescriptions of the Code on clerical dress as contained in canon 136, § 1, are very general. All that the Code prescribes is that the dress be a fitting one, that is, one that conforms to the dignity of the clerical state. Everything else is left to the determination of local customs and the prescriptions of the ordinary. This is substantially the same prescription as was contained in the Council of Trent.[38] It is not necessary, then, that the ecclesiastical dress be the cassock unless local custom or the ordinary prescribes the cassock. When the cassock is not prescribed, the dress is usually a garment of a black color, but it

---

[36] Conc. Trident., sess. XIV, *de ref.*, c. 6; Sixtus V, const. "*Cum sacrosanctam,*" 9 ian. 1589—*Fontes,* n. 167; Benedictus XIII, const. "*In supremo,*" 23 sept. 1724—*Fontes,* n. 283; const. "*Apostolicae Ecclesiae,*" 2 maii 1725—*Fontes,* n. 286; Pius IX, ep. encycl. "*Nemo certe ignorat,*" 25 mart. 1852—*Fontes,* n. 514.

[37] Toso, *Commentaria Minora,* II, 99.

[38] Sess. XIV, *de ref.*, c. 6.

may also be of another color if the circumstances warrant it.[39] In the United States of America the II and III Plenary Councils of Baltimore have prescribed that the roman collar and a black coat extending to the knees is the proper garb to be worn by the clergy in civil life.[40] The prescription that the coat extend in length to the knees has been abrogated by a contrary custom which has at least the tacit approval of the Holy See and of the bishops.[41]

An instruction of the Sacred Congregation of the Council has emphasized the necessity of wearing the proper ecclesiastical garb whenever a cleric appears in public even during the time of the summer vacation.[42] If a cleric visits another diocese, he may retain the ecclesiastical dress of his own diocese, provided that he has no domicile or quasi-domicile in the diocese which he is visiting; on the other hand, he may also wear the ecclesiastical garb of the diocese which he is visiting, and his own ordinary may not reprehend him for this.[43] While this interpretation is based on a declaration which was given before the Code by the Sacred Consistorial Congregation to a particular territory, Canada, yet the principles involved are still applicable after the Code.

With the foregoing short review of these few general ideas on ecclesiastical dress it is possible to treat of the tacit renunciation sanctioned in canon 188, n. 7. This canon states that a cleric loses his office by a tacit renunciation if on his own authority and without a just cause he doffs his ecclesiastical

---

[39] S. C. de Prop. Fide, instr. (pro Mission. Malabar.), 9 apr. 1783—*Fontes*, n. 4595.

[40] *Concilii Plenarii Baltimorensis II, in Ecclesia Metropolitana Baltimorensi, a die VII ad diem XXI Octobris, A. D. MDCCCLXVI, habiti, et a Sede Apostolica Recogniti, Acta et Decreta* (Baltimorae, 1868), nn. 147–149; *Acta et Decreta Concilii Plenarii Baltimorensis Tertii, A. D. MDCCCLXXXIV* (Baltimorae, 1894), n. 77.

[41] Barrett, *A Comparative Study of the Councils of Baltimore and the Code of Canon Law,* The Catholic University of America Canon Law Studies, n. 83 (Washington, D. C.: The Catholic University of America, 1932), pp. 48–49.

[42] 28 iul. 1931—*AAS*, XXIII (1931), 336–337.

[43] S. C. Consist., declar. 31 mart. 1916—*AAS*, VII (1916), 148–150.

garb and does not resume it within a month after he has received a warning from the ordinary. As Cocchi remarks,[44] all these elements must be present in order to effect the tacit renunciation. In the first place, the cleric must remove his ecclesiastical garb on his own authority and without a just cause. If he should do so with the permission of the ordinary or on the authority of another legitimate superior, his act would not constitute a juridical basis for a tacit renunciation. Even if he should do so on his own authority, his act would not call for the application of the sanction enacted in canon 188, n. 7, if there were present a righteous cause to justify such action. Thus, for instance, a cleric could find it necessary in some given circumstances to remove his ecclesiastical garb for a period of time in order to minister spiritual aid to his people without being disturbed by enemies of the faith. If the cleric were placed in such circumstances, certainly he would have a just cause for doffing the clerical garb. It must be remembered, however, that it pertains to the ordinary to judge whether or not the alleged cause is just.[45]

The fact that a cleric has removed his clerical garb on his own authority without a just cause is still not sufficient to effect the tacit renunciation of his office. Canon 188, n. 7, further postulates that the ordinary have issued a warning, upon which for an entire month the cleric still has not resumed the wearing of the ecclesiastical garb, before the tacit renunciation will take effect. The warning should be issued by the ordinary in such a way that he will be able to certify the fact that the cleric has received it, for the month's time begins to lapse only after the cleric has received the warning. For this purpose the warning should be given orally before the chancellor or before two witnesses, or in writing by means of a registered letter with a return receipt certifying the arrival of the letter, or by some other safe means of correspondence.[46] Since the time does not begin to run its course until the warning has been received by the cleric, the time to be computed is of the nature of available

[44] *Commentarium,* II, n. 101.

[45] Toso, *op. cit.,* II, 156.

[46] Cf. can. 2143, § 1; 1719.

time "*ratione initii.*"[47] But it is not clear from the text of the law whether thenceforth the month's duration of time is to be measured (1) continuously, that is, without regard for any temporal intermission during which the cleric may either not be able, or in law not be held, to wear the ecclesiastical garb, or (2) only intermittently, that is, solely with relation to such time during which the cleric has both the given opportunity and at the same time the duty in law to wear the distinctive clerical dress. Coronata[48] and Blat[49] maintain that the month's duration as here involved is to be computed in the nature of a continuous time, while Toso[50] considers that the course of the month's time is to be reckoned in accordance with the lapse of only such time during which the cleric has the available opportunity of complying with what strict law demands of him in the wearing of the clerical garb. The latter opinion seems to be in closer harmony with the demand of canonical equity, for, as Toso remarks,[51] a just cause for not wearing the clerical garb may be present during the current calendar month, and such a circumstance seems to interrupt the continuity of the course of the month's duration. If the month is actually continuous, that is, no excusing just cause is present during the month, then the month is computed as a calendar month, and accordingly the time expires with the completion of the last day with an identical date. If an impediment occurs during the month, then the time is computed as thirty days of twenty-four hours each. In order that a person be considered as impeded from acting for a day's time, it seems sufficient that the impediment hinder the person for a notable part of the day.[52]

If the cleric wears the clerical garb for merely an hour in order to circumvent the law, such an act would not constitute a resumption of the clerical garb. If, however, he seriously resumes

---

[47] Cf. Dubé, *The General Principles for the Reckoning of Time in Canon Law*, pp. 230–233.

[48] *Institutiones*, I, n. 263.

[49] *Commentarium*, II, n. 135.

[50] *Commentaria Minora*, II, 156.

[51] *Loc. cit.*

[52] Cf. Dubé, *op. cit.*, pp. 233–240

the proper dress, even though the period of time during which he retains it is of short duration, a new warning on the part of the ordinary would be necessary, and the cleric would have another month's time at his disposal.[53] If the cleric fails to resume the proper ecclesiastical dress within an available period of time equal to the duration of a month after he has received the warning of the ordinary, his office becomes automatically vacant in consequence of the tacit renunciation sanctioned in canon 188, n. 7.

Article IV. Desertion of Residence

> Can. 188, n. 8. [*Si clericus*] *Residentiam qua tenetur, illegitime deseruerit et receptae Ordinarii monitioni, legitimo impedimento non detentus, intra congruum tempus ab Ordinario praefinitum, nec paruerit nec responderit.*

Residence in general is the remaining or abiding in the place where one's duties lie or where one's occupation is properly carried on.[54] It is a merely material residence when a person is indeed corporeally present in the place of his duties but does nothing by way of performing them. It is a formal residence when the person is not only actually present but also performs the duties incumbent upon him. Although a formal residence is necessary for constituting a true residence, nevertheless the present canon is directed against the violation of material residence alone.[55]

Prior to the Code the obligation of residence was attached to all offices which had annexed to them the care of souls, and also to the offices in a cathedral or a collegiate chapter. All other offices had no obligation of residence, unless the obligation was attached to them by custom or by particular law.[56] The obligation of residence was a serious obligation, and those who violated it were subjected to the penalty of privation of the fruits of the

---

[53] Blat, *Commentarium,* II, n. 135.

[54] Reilly, *Residence of Pastors,* The Catholic University of America Canon Law Studies, n. 97 (Washington, D. C.: The Catholic University of America, 1935), p. 3.

[55] *Ibid.,* p. 48.

[56] Henry, *De Residentia Beneficiatorum* (Lovanii, 1863), pp. 3-4; 222-227.

benefice, and subsequently to the penalty of privation of the benefice itself.[57]

The Code has maintained in substance the pre-Code standard with reference to the obligation of residence. This obligation is attached by law to offices in the strict sense which have annexed to them the care of souls, as, for example, the offices of the residential bishop,[58] of the pastor,[59] of the parochial vicar administrator [60] and of the actual parochial vicar.[61] Besides, the Code attaches the obligation of residence to the office of cathedral or collegiate canons [62] and to the office of a cardinal.[63] Even if the Code does not attach the obligation of residence to an office, the office may still entail that obligation by reason of custom or of particular law.

Canon 188, n. 8, states that a cleric who illegitimately deserts the residence incumbent upon him and does not either answer or obey the warning of the ordinary within the time prescribed by the ordinary, loses his office through a tacit renunciation of it. Some authors maintain that the sanction of canon 188, n. 8, takes effect not only in the face of a neglect of the obligation of residence which is annexed to an office, but also in the face of a violation of the law of canon 143 which forbids a cleric to leave the diocese for a notable period of time without at least the presumed permission of the ordinary.[64] Thus according to these authors a cleric who has an office with no special obligation of residence attached to it would nevertheless lose his office through a tacit renunciation of it if he violated canon 143, and thereupon neither answered nor obeyed the ordinary's warning within the prescribed time. Others hold that canon 188, n. 8, has

---

[57] Conc. Trident., sess. VI, *de ref.*, cc. 1–2; sess. XXIII, *de ref.*, c. 1; sess. XXIV, *de ref.*, c. 12.

[58] Can. 338.

[59] Can. 465.

[60] Can. 473, § 1.

[61] Can. 471, § 4.

[62] Can. 418, § 1; 419, § 1; 420–421.

[63] Can. 238.

[64] Coronata, *Institutiones*, I, p. 302, footnote 1; Cocchi, *Commentarium*, II, n. 101.

reference only to the obligation of residence as attached to the office which the cleric possesses.[65]

The writer favors the latter opinion. Canon 143 treats of residence only in the broadest sense of the term, while the tenor of canon 188, n. 8, seems to demand a residence which is attached in a special manner to the office which the cleric possesses. Canon 2168, which introduces the rules governing the administrative removal of non-resident clerics, and canon 2381, which contains the penalties against non-resident clerics, expressly mention that the obligation of residence which is under consideration in these canons is that which binds the clerics by reason of a conferred office, benefice or dignity. Canon 188, n. 8, has a very definite relationship to these canons. As a matter of fact canon 188, n. 8, constitutes the initial step in the administrative procedure outlined in canons 2168–2175. Hence the writer believes that canon 188, n. 8, like the other canons just mentioned, should be restricted in its application so that it will point solely to the violation of the obligation of residence which as a duty binds a cleric by reason of the office he possesses.

If a cleric who possesses an office with the obligation of residence annexed to it should violate the law of canon 143 by leaving the diocese for a notable period of time without at least the presumed permission of the ordinary, he would almost inevitably violate also the obligation of residence attached to his office, since the latter obligation seems ordinarily the stricter of the two. If, however, he possesses an office which has no special obligation of residence attached to it, then the violation of the law of canon 143 would not constitute a foundation for the tacit renunciation effectively sanctioned in canon 188, n. 8.

The obligation of residence prescribed in canon 143 is only very remotely connected with the office. Even if a cleric should resume the residence prescribed in canon 143, he could remain in any remote part of the diocese without reporting to the place where his non-residential office exists. Canon 188, n. 8, on the other hand, seems to have reference to an obligation of residence which is proximately connected with the cleric's office. Hence

---

[65] Blat, *Commentarium,* II, n. 135; Toso, *Commentaria Minora,* II, 156.

the writer believes that a tacit renunciation is effected only by the violation of obligation of that residence which binds a cleric by reason of the office he possesses. Violations of canon 143 should be provided for in accordance with the prescriptions of canon 2399, which states that a major cleric who presumes to abandon a charge committed to him by the ordinary is to be suspended "*a divinis*" for a period of time to be defined by the ordinary according to the need inherent in each particular case.

According to canon 188, n. 8, a cleric who is illegitimately absent, and fails either to answer or to obey the ordinary's warning within the prescribed time, loses his office through a tacit renunciation of it. In the first place, then, the absence must be illegitimate, that is, contrary to what the law permits to the incumbent. It may be illegitimate with reference either to the duration of the absence or to the manner of taking leave from one's residence. Thus, a pastor would be illegitimately absent from his parish if he should leave for more than a week without obtaining the ordinary's written permission when there is sufficient time to consult the ordinary.[66] It is necessary to consult the prescriptions of both the common and the particular law in order to determine when a specific absence is illegitimate.

It is necessary also that the ordinary have warned the cleric of his violation. This warning must be issued either orally before the chancellor, or before some other official of the curia, or before two witnesses, or in writing by means of a registered letter with a receipt certifying the arrival of the letter, or by some other safe means of correspondence.[67] In the warning the ordinary should call the cleric's attention to the penalties enacted in law against non-resident clerics, and also to the prescriptions of canon 188, n. 8, and he must further indicate to the cleric that he is to resume residence within a specified fitting period of time.[68] The period of time allowed for the cleric for resuming his residence must be a fitting period of time, and therefore it will vary according to the circumstances of each in-

---

[66] Can. 465, § 4.

[67] Can. 2143; 1719.

[68] Can. 2168, § 2.

dividual case. The period of granted time is necessarily of the nature of available time since the canon excuses the cleric if a legitimate impediment prevents him from answering or obeying the warning of the ordinary.[69]

If the cleric does not resume his residence, or at least answer the ordinary's warning within the specified time, the office becomes vacant automatically by reason of the cleric's tacit renunciation of it. Canon 2169 states that the ordinary is to declare the office vacant when he has been assured that the cleric has received the warning and was not legitimately impeded from answering it. As Reilly notes,[70] this declaration is not a necessary condition for the vacancy since the office becomes vacant through a tacit renunciation which needs no declaration of the superior to complete it for the sake of achieving its juridical effect. The ordinary should, however, make the proper investigation to assure himself that the warning was received by the cleric, and that he was not impeded from answering it, for if either of these conditions is not verified, then the tacit renunciation does not take effect, and accordingly the office can not be validly conferred upon another. If there exists any doubt about these matters, the ordinary must repeat the warning[71] If it is clear that the warning was received, and that the cleric, in no way legitimately impeded, failed either to answer the warning or obey it within the specified time, the office becomes vacant automatically through the cleric's tacit renunciation of it and may then be conferred to another.

It is to be noted that the tacit renunciation takes place only if the cleric neither obeys the warning nor answers it. If the cleric resumes residence after his illegitimate absence, the ordinary must punish him with the deprivation of the fruits of his office for the time of his absence in accordance with the prescriptions of canon 2381, and, if the case calls for it, he may punish him also with other penalties in proportion to his guilt.[72]

---

[69] Can. 188, n. 8; 35.

[70] *Residence of Pastors*, p. 51.

[71] Can. 2149.

[72] Can. 2170.

If the cleric does not resume residence, but answers the ordinary by alleging the reasons for his absence, then the administrative procedure as outlined in canons 2168–2175 is to be continued to the point which will warrant the issuance of an authoritative decree at the hands of the ordinary.

CONCLUSIONS

1. The rules which regulate the renunciation of an ecclesiastical office apply to the renunciation of an ecclesiastical office to which the cleric has a *ius in re,* even though he has not taken possession of the office.

2. A minor may renounce an ecclesiastical office without the consent of his parents or tutors.

3. The ordinary may prohibit the renunciation of any one or all ecclesiastical offices under his jurisdiction whenever in his judgment the needs of the Church demand such a prohibition.

4. The vicar capitular or, in places where there is no Cathedral Chapter, the diocesan administrator and the temporary apostolic administrator appointed to a vacant see may admit the renunciation of all offices in the territory with the exception (1) of parochial benefices of free conferral within the first year of the vacancy of the see, and (2) of all perpetual benefices of free conferral.

5. Whenever it is required for the validity of a resignation that the superior accept the resignation, the resignation is invalid if unjustly inspired grave fear, deceit, substantial error, or simony vitiates the superior's act of acceptance.

6. Both substantial and accidental deceit render a resignation invalid.

7. An incumbent may revoke his resignation provided that he notify the superior of this intention before he has received the notification of the superior's acceptance of his resignation.

8. A tacit renunciation of an ecclesiastical office is not a presumed resignation; it is a true resignation admitted by the law as equivalent to an express renunciation.

9. A tacit renunciation of an ecclesiastical office is not a penalty, even though some of the acts which effect such a renunciation are criminal acts. Therefore, Cardinals are subject to the prescriptions of canon 188.

10. Whenever the Holy See confers a second incompatible office upon a cleric, the conferral of the second office is invalid unless there is mention of the prior incompatible office in the petition for the second office, or unless there is a derogating clause in the rescript of conferral of the second office. Even though there is mention of the prior incompatible office in the petition, or even though a derogating clause is contained in the rescript, the cleric loses his first office through a tacit renunciation of it when he takes peaceful possession of the second office, unless a special dispensation from the rule enacted in canon 188, n. 3, is granted to him.

BIBLIOGRAPHY

SOURCES

Acta Apostolicae Sedis, Commentarium Officiale, Romae, 1909–

Acta et Decreta Concilii Plenarii Baltimorensis Tertii, A. D. MDCCCLXXXIV, Baltimorae, 1894.

Acta Sanctae Sedis, 41 vols., Romae, 1865–1908.

Bullarum Diplomatum et Privilegiorum Romanorum Pontificum Taurinensis Editio, 25 vols., Augustae Taurinorum, 1857–1872.

Canones et Decreta Sacrosancti et Oecumenici Concilii Tridentini, Parisiis, 1754.

Codex Iuris Canonici Pii X Pontificis Maximi iussu digestus, Benedicti Papae XV auctoritate promulgatus, Romae: Typis Polyglottis Vaticanis, 1917. Reimpressio, 1933.

Codicis Iuris Canonici Fontes cura Emi Petri Card. Gasparri editi, 9 vols., Romae: Typis Polyglottis Vaticanis, 1923–1939. (Vols. VII–IX ed. cura et studio Emi Iustiniani Serédi.)

Concilii Plenarii Baltimorensis II, in Ecclesia Metropolitana Baltimorensi, a die VII ad diem XXI Octobris, A. D. *MDCCCLXVI, habiti, et a Sede Apostolica Recogniti, Acta et Decreta,* Baltimorae, 1868.

Continuatio Bullarii Romani Benedicti XIV, 3 vols. in 4, Prati, 1845–1847.

Corpus Iuris Canonici, ed. Lipsiensis 2. post Aemilii Ludovici Richteri curas . . . instruxit Aemilius Friedberg, Lipsiae: Ex Officina Bernhardi Tauchnitz, 1879–1881. Editio anastatice repetita, Lipsiae: Tauchnitz, 1928.

Corpus Iuris Civilis, Vol. I, ed. stereotypa quinta decima, *Institutiones,* recognovit Paulus Krueger, *Digesta* recognovit Theodorus Mommsen, retractavit Paulus Krueger, Berolini: Apud Weidmannos, 1928.

Decretales D. Gregorii IX una cum Glossis Restitutae, Romae, 1582.

Decretum Gratiani Emendatum et notationibus illustratum una cum Glossis, Gregorii XIII. Pont. Max. iussu editum, 2 vols., Romae, 1582.

Jaffé, Philippus, *Regesta Pontificum Romanorum ab condita Ecclesia ad annum post Christum natum MCXCVIII,* ed. 2. correctam et auctam auspiciis Gulielmi Wattenbach curaverunt S. Loewenfeld, F. Kaltenbrunner, P. Ewald, 2 vols. in 1, Lipsiae, 1885–1888.

Liber Sextus Decretalium D. Bonifatii Papae VIII suae integritati una cum Clementinis et Extravagantibus earumque Glossis restitutis, Romae, 1582.

Mansi, Joannes Dominicus, *Sacrorum Conciliorum Nova et Amplissima Collectio,* 53 vols. in 60, Paris-Arnhem-Leipzig, 1901–1927.

Pallottini, Salvator, *Collectio Omnium Conclusionum et Resolutionum Quae in causis propositis apud Sacram Congregationem Cardinalium S. Concilii Tridentini Interpretum Prodierunt ab eius institutione, anno MDLXIV ad MDCCCLX distinctis titulis alphabetico ordine per materias digestas,* 18 vols., Romae, 1868–1893.

Potthast, Augustus, *Regesta Pontificum Romanorum inde ab anno post Christum natum MCXCVIII ad annum MCCCIV,* 2 vols., Berolini, 1874–1875.

Sacrae Romanae Rotae decisiones recentiores, ed. Farinacius, Rubeus, et Compagnus, 25 vols., Venetiis, 1697.

Thesaurus Resolutionum Sacrae Congregationis Concilii, 167 vols., Romae, 1718–1908.

REFERENCE WORKS

Ayrinhac, H. A.-Lydon, P. J., *Penal Legislation in the New Code of Canon Law,* 2. ed., New York: Benziger Brothers, 1936.

(Bachofen), Charles Augustine, *A Commentary on the New Code of Canon Law,* 8 vols., Vol. II, 6. ed., 1936; Vol. VI, 3. ed., 1931; Vol. VIII, 3. ed., 1931, St. Louis: Herder Book Co.

Barbosa, Augustine, *Collectanea Doctorum tam veterum quam recentiorum in Jus Pontificium Universum,* 6 vols. in 3, Lugduni, 1669.

———, *De Officio et Potestate Episcopi,* 3 vols. in 1, Lugduni, 1628.

Barrett, John, *A Comparative Study of the Councils of Baltimore and the Code of Canon Law,* The Catholic University of America Canon Law Studies, n. 83, Washington, D. C.: The Catholic University of America, 1932.

Benko, Matthew, *The Abbot Nullius,* The Catholic University of America Canon Law Studies, n. 173, Washington, D. C.: The Catholic University of America Press, 1943.

Beste, Udalricus, *Introductio in Codićem,* ed. altera, Collegeville, Minn.: St. John's Abbey Press, 1944.

Blat, Albertus, *Commentarium Textus Codicis Iuris Canonici,* 5 vols. in 6, Vol. II, 2. ed., 1921; Vol. III, Pars altera, 1923, Romae: F. Ferrari.

Bouix, D., *Tractatus de iure Regularium,* 2 vols., Parisiis, 1857.

Campagna, Angelo, *Il Vicario Generale del Vescovo,* The Catholic University of America Canon Law Studies, n. 66, Washington, D. C.: The Catholic University of America, 1931.

Cappello, Felix, *Summa Iuris Canonici,* 3 vols., Vol I, 3. ed., 1938, Romae: Apud Aedes Universitatis Gregorianae.

———, *Tractatus Canonico-Moralis de Censuris iuxta Codicem Iuris Canonici,* 3. ed., Taurini: Marietti, 1933.

———, *Tractatus Canonico-Moralis de Sacramentis,* 3 vols., Vol. III, *De Matrimonio,* 3. ed., 1933, Taurinorum Augustae: Marietti.

Castillo, Cayo, *Disertacion Historico-Canonico sobre la Podestad del Cabildo en Sede Vacante o Impedida del Vicario Capitular,* The Catholic

University of America Canon Law Studies, n. 4, Washington, D. C.: The Catholic University of America, 1919.

Cerato, P., *Censurae Vigentes Ipso Facto a Codice Iuris Canonici Excerptae,* 2. ed., Patavii, 1921.

Chelodi, Ioannes, *Ius de Personis,* ed. altera a Sac. Ernesto Bertagnolli, Tridenti: Libr. Edit. Tridentum, 1927.

Cipollini, Albertus, *De Censuris Latae Sententiae iuxta Codicem Iuris Canonici,* 2 vols. in 1, Taurini: Marietti, 1925.

Claeys Bouuaert, F.–Simenon, G., *Manuale Juris Canonici,* 3 vols., Vol. I, 3. ed., 1930, Gandae et Leodii: Seminarium Gandavense et Leodiense.

Cocchi, Guidus, *Commentarium in Codicem Iuris Canonici,* 8 vols., Vol. II, 4. ed., 1937; Vol. VIII, 4. ed., 1938, Taurinorum Augustae: Marietti.

Connors, Charles, *Extra-judicial Procurators in the Code of Canon Law,* The Catholic University of America Canon Law Studies, n. 192, Washington, D. C.: The Catholic University of America Press, 1944.

Coronata, Matthaeus Conte a, *Institutiones Iuris Canonici,* 5 vols., Vol. I, 1928; Vol. IV, 1935, Taurini: Marietti.

———, *Ius Publicum Ecclesiasticum,* 2. ed., Taurini: Marietti, 1934.

De Angelis, Philippus, *Praelectiones Iuris Canonici, ad Methodum Decretalium Gregorii IX Exactae,* 4 vols. in 6, Romae, 1877–1887.

Dillon, Robert, *Common Law Marriage,* The Catholic University of America Canon Law Studies, n. 153, Washington, D. C.: The Catholic University of America Press, 1942.

Downs, John, *The Concept of Clerical Immunity,* The Catholic University of America Canon Law Studies, n. 126, Washington, D. C.: The Catholic University of America Press, 1941.

Dubé, Arthur, *The General Principles for the Reckoning of Time in Canon Law,* The Catholic University of America Canon Law Studies, n. 144, Washington, D. C.: The Catholic University of America Press, 1941.

Fagnanus, Prosper, *Commentaria in Quinque Libros Decretalium,* 3 vols., Venetiis, 1709.

Garcia, Nicolaus, *Tractatus de Beneficiis,* Coloniae Allobrogum, 1636.

Gennari, Casimiro Card., *Sulla Privazione del Beneficio Ecclesiastico e sul Processo Criminale dei Chierici,* 2. ed., Romae, 1905.

Gonzalez-Tellez, Manuel, *Commentaria Perpetua in singulos textus Quinque Librorum Decretalium Gregorii IX,* 5 vols. in 4, Venetiis, 1699.

Haydt, John, *Reserved Benefices,* The Catholic University of America Canon Law Studies, n. 161, Washington, D. C.: The Catholic University of America Press, 1942.

Heneghan, John, *The Marriage of Unworthy Catholics, Canons 1065 and 1066,* The Catholic University of America Canon Law Studies, n. 188, Washington, D. C.: The Catholic University of America Press, 1944.

Henry, Ludovicus, *De Residentia Beneficiatorum,* Lovanii, 1863.

Hostiensis, Cardinalis (Henricus de Segusio), *Commentaria in Quinque Decretalium Libros,* 5 vols. in 3, Venetiis, 1581.

Ioannes Andreae, *Commentaria in Quinque Decretalium Libros Novella,* Venetiis, 1581.

Klekotka, Peter, *Diocesan Consultors,* The Catholic University of America Canon Law Studies, n. 8, Washington, D. C.: The Catholic University of America, 1920.

Lega, Michael, *De Iudiciis Ecclesiasticis,* 4 vols., Vol. III, 1899, Romae.

Leurenius, Peter, *Forum Beneficiale,* 4 partes in 2, Venetiis, 1742.

MacKenzie, Eric, *The Delict of Heresy in its Commission, Penalization, Absolution,* The Catholic University of America Canon Law Studies, n. 77, Washington, D. C.: The Catholic University of America, 1932.

McBride, James, *Incardination and Excardination of Seculars,* The Catholic University of America Canon Law Studies, n. 145, Washington, D. C.: The Catholic University of America Press, 1941.

McDonough, Thomas, *Apostolic Administrators,* The Catholic University of America Canon Law Studies, n. 139, Washington, D. C.: The Catholic University of America Press, 1941.

Maroto, Philippus, *Institutiones Iuris Canonici ad Normam Novi Codicis,* 2 vols., Vol. I, 3. ed., 1921, Romae: Apud Commentarium pro Religiosis.

Michaels, Gommarus, *De Delictis et Poenis,* Vol. I, Lublin: Universitas Catholica, 1934.

Noldin, H.-Schmitt, A., *Summa Theologiae Moralis,* 3 vols., Vol. I, 27. ed., 1940, Oeniponte: Rauch.

Panormitanus, Abbas (Nicolaus de Tudeschis), *Commentaria in Quinque Decretalium Libros,* 5 vols. in 7, Venetiis, 1588.

Pirhing, Ernricus, *Jus Canonicum Nova Methodo Explicatum,* 5 vols. in 4, Dilingae, 1674–1678.

Pistocchi, Marius, *De re beneficiali,* Taurini: Marietti, 1928.

Raymundus de Pennafort, *Summa,* Veronae, 1744.

Reiffenstuel, Anacletus, *Jus Canonicum Universum,* 5 vols. in 7, Parisiis, 1864–1882.

Reilly, Peter, *Residence of Pastors,* The Catholic University of America Canon Law Studies, n. 97, Washington, D. C.: The Catholic University of America, 1935.

Riganti, Ioannes B., *Commentaria in regulas, constitutiones, et ordinationes Cancellariae Apostolicae,* 4 vols. in 2, Coloniae Allobrogum, 1751.

Roelker, Edward, *Principles of Privilege according to the Code of Canon Law,* The Catholic University of America Canon Law Studies, n. 35, Washington, D. C.: The Catholic University of America, 1926.

Ryder, Raymond, *Simony,* The Catholic University of America Canon Law Studies, n. 65, Washington, D. C.: The Catholic University of America, 1931.

Sanchez, Thomas, *De Sancto Matrimonio Disputationum Libri Decem, in Tres Tomos Distributi,* Venetiis, 1712.

Santi, Franciscus, *Praelectiones Iuris Canonici,* 2 vols., Ratisbonae, Neo-Eboraci, Cincinnati, 1886.

Schäfer, Timothacus, *Compendium de Religiosis ad Normam Codicis Juris Canonici,* 2. ed., Münster i. W.: Ex Officini Libraria Aschendorf, 1931.

Schmalzgrueber, Franciscus, *Jus Ecclesiasticum Universum,* 5 vols. in 12, Romae, 1843–1845.

Sipos, Stephanus, *Enchiridion Juris Canonici,* 3. ed., Pécs: Ex Typographia "Haladás R. T.," 1936.

Smith, Mariner, *The Penal Law for Religious,* The Catholic University of America Canon Law Studies, n. 98, Washington, D. C.: The Catholic University of America, 1935.

Toso, Albertus, *Ad Codicem Iuris Canonici Commentaria Minora,* 5 vols., Vol. II, 1921, Romae: Marietti.

Vermeersch A.-Creusen, J., *Epitome Iuris Canonici,* 3 vols., Vol. I, 6. ed., 1937; Vol. III, 5. ed., 1936, Mechliniae: H. Dessain.

Wernz, Franciscus, X., *Ius Decretalium,* 6 vols., Vol. II, 3. ed. 1915, Prati.

Wernz, F. X.-Vidal, P., *Ius Canonicum,* 7 vols. in 8, Vol. II, 2. ed., 1928, Romae: Apud Aedes Universitatis Gregorianae.

Winslow, Francis, *Vicars and Prefects Apostolic,* The Catholic University of America Canon Law Studies, n. 24, Washington, D. C.: The Catholic University of America, 1924.

Woywod, Stanislaus, *A Practical Commentary on the Code of Canon Law,* 2 vols., Vol. I, 7. ed., revised by Callistus Smith, 1943, New York: Joseph F. Wagner.

PERIODICALS

Analecta Ecclesiastica, Romae, 1893–1911.

Analecta Iuris Pontificii, Romae, 1855–1869; Parisiis, 1872–1891.

Archiv für katholisches Kirchenrecht, Innsbruck, 1857–1861; Mainz, 1862–

Apollinaris, Romae, 1928–

Jurist, The, Washington, D. C., 1941–

Jus Pontificium, Romae, 1921–

Monitore Ecclesiastico, Il, Romae, 1876–

Periodica de Re Canonica et Morali utilia praesertim Religiosis et Missionariis, Bruges, 1905– ; ab anno 1927: *Periodica de Re Morali, Canonica, Liturgica.*

Revue Ecclésiastique de Liège, Liège, 1908–

ARTICLES

Anonymous, "Traité des Résignations"—*Analecta Iuris Pontificii,* II (1857), 1486–1533.

Cappello, F., "De beneficio possesso a candidato qui religionem ingreditur" —*Periodica,* XXII (1933), 202–209.

———, "De vacatione beneficii post emissam professionem religiosam"— *Periodica,* XXII (1933), 101–108.

Gillet, P., "De actione rescissoria ob dolum"—*Jus Pontificium*, IX (1929), 323–324.

Gillmann, F., "Die Resignation der Benefizien"—*AKKR*, LXX (1900), 523–569.

Hilling, N., "Kirchliches *Officium* und *Potestas ordinaria*"—*AKKR*, CXVII (1937), 433–435.

Mostaza, M., "De simonia confidentiali in Codice Iur. Can., deque requisitis in quovis delicto simoniae ex parte actus ad poenas canonicas contrahendas—*Periodica*, XX (1931), 118–125.

Roberti, F., "De actione rescissoria ob dolum"—*Apollinaris*, III (1930), 143–144.

Salsmans, I., "Circa Vitia Consensus"—*Jus Pontificium*, X (1930), 104–109.

Simenon, G., "Renuntiatio Officiorum Ecclesiasticorum"—*Revue Ecclésiastique de Liège*, XXII (1930–1931), 182–186.

Sipos, S., "Ad officium sacrum an requiritur potestas ordinaria"—*Jus Pontificium*, XVI (1936), 67–68.

ABBREVIATIONS

AAS—*Acta Apostolicae Sedis.*
AKKR—*Archiv für katholisches Kirchenrecht.*
ASS—*Acta Sanctae Sedis.*
Bullarium—*Bullarum Diplomatum . . . Romanorum Pontificum Taurinensis Editio.*
Can.—Canon.
D.—Digestum (Iustinianum).
Fontes—*Codicis Iuris Canonici Fontes cura . . . Gasparri editi.*
Jaffé—*Regesta Pontificum Romanorum, etc.*
Mansi—*Sacrorum Conciliorum Nova et Amplissima Collectio.*
P.C.I.—*Pontificia Commissio ad Codicis Canones Authentice Interpretandos.*
Periodica—*Periodica de Re Morali, Canonica, Liturgica, etc.*
Potthast—*Regesta Pontificum Romanorum, etc.*
S. C. C.—Sacra Congregatio Concilii.
S. C. de Prop. Fide—Sacra Congregatio de Propaganda Fide.
S. C. S. Off.—Suprema Congregatio Sancti Officii.

INDEX

BIOGRAPHICAL NOTE

Gerald Vincent McDevitt was born on February 23, 1917, at Philadelphia, Pennsylvania. He attended Our Mother of Sorrows Parochial School and La Salle College High School of that city. In September of 1932 he was admitted into the Seminary of St. Charles Borromeo, Philadelphia, where he completed his preparatory studies and his course in Philosophy. In August of 1938 he was sent to pursue his Theological Studies at the Pontifical Roman Seminary, Rome, Italy. He received the degree of S. T. B. from the Pontificio Ateneo Lateranense in May of 1940. The following September he entered the Theological College of the Catholic University of America where he received the degree of S. T. L. in May, 1942. He was ordained to the Holy Priesthood on May 30, 1942, at Philadelphia. In the fall of that year he enrolled in the School of Canon Law of the Catholic University of America, where he received the degree of J. C. B. in May, 1943, and the degree of J. C. L. in May, 1944.

CANON LAW STUDIES

1. FRERIKS, REV. CELESTINE A. C.PP.S., J.C.D., Religious Congregations in Their External Relations, 121 pp., 1916.
2. GALLIHER, REV. DANIEL M., O.P., J.C.D., Canonical Elections, 117 pp., 1917.
3. BORKOWSKI, REV. AURELIUS L., O.F.M., J.C.D., De Confraternitatibus Ecclesiasticis, 136 pp., 1918.
4. CASTILLO, REV. CAYO, J.C.D., Disertacion Historico-Canonica sobre la Potestad del Cabildo en Sede Vacante o Impedida del Vicario Capitular, 99 pp., 1919 (1918).
5. KUBELBECK, REV. WILLIAM J., S.T.B., J.C.D., The Sacred Penitentiaria and Its Relation to Faculties of Ordinaries and Priests, 129 pp., 1918.
6. PETROVITS, REV. JOSEPH, J. C., S.T.D., J.C.D., The New Church Law on Matrimony, X-461 pp., 1919.
7. HICKEY, REV. JOHN J., S.T.B., J.C.D., Irregularities and Simple Impediments in the New Code of Canon Law, 100 pp., 1920.
8. KLEKOTKA, REV. PETER J., S.T.B., J.C.D., Diocesan Consultors, 179 pp., 1920.
9. WANENMACHER, REV. FRANCIS, J.C.D., The Evidence in Ecclesiastical Procedure Affecting the Marriage Bond, 1920 (Printed 1935).
10. GOLDEN, REV. HENRY FRANCIS, J.C.D., Parochial Benefices in the New Code, IV-119 pp., 1921 (Printed 1925).
11. KOUDELKA, REV. CHARLES J., J.C.D., Pastors, Their Rights and Duties According to the New Code of Canon Law, 211 pp., 1921.
12. MELO, REV. ANTONIUS, O.F.M., J.C.D., De Exemptione Regularium, X-188 pp., 1921.
13. SCHAAF, REV. VALENTINE THEODORE, O.F.M., S.T.B., J.C.D., The Cloister, X-180 pp., 1921.
14. BURKE, REV. THOMAS JOSEPH, S.T.D., J.C.D., Competence in Ecclesiastical Tribunals, IV-117 pp., 1922.
15. LEECH, REV. GEORGE LEO, J.C.D., A Comparative Study of the Constitution "Apostolicae Sedis" and the "Codex Juris Canonici," 179 pp., 1922.
16. MOTRY, REV. HUBERT LOUIS, S.T.D., J.C.D., Diocesan Faculties According to the Code of Canon Law, II-167 pp., 1922.
17. MURPHY, REV. GEORGE LAWRENCE, J.C.D., Delinquencies and Penalties in the Administration and the Reception of the Sacraments, IV-121 pp., 1923.

* Below n. 100 only the following numbers are still available: Nos. 25, 57 and 75. Beginning with n. 100 only the following numbers are unavailable: Nos. 100–111 inclusive, 113 and 115–117 inclusive.

18. O'Reilly, Rev. John Anthony, S.T.B., J.C.D., Ecclesiastical Sepulture in the New Code of Canon Law, II-129 pp., 1923.
19. Michalicka, Rev. Wenceslas Cyril, O.S.B., J.C.D., Judicial Procedure in Dismissal of Clerical Exempt Religious, 107 pp., 1923.
20. Dargin, Rev. Edward Vincent, S.T.B., J.C.D., Reserved Cases According to the Code of Canon Law, IV-103 pp., 1924.
21. Godfrey, Rev. John A., S.T.B., J.C.D., The Right of Patronage According to the Code of Canon Law, 153 pp., 1924.
22. Hagedorn, Rev. Francis Edward, J.C.D., General Legislation on Indulgences, II-154 pp., 1924.
23. King, Rev. James Ignatius, J.C.D., The Administration of the Sacraments to Dying Non-Catholics, V-141 pp., 1924.
24. Winslow, Rev. Francis Joseph, O.F.M., J.C.D., Vicars and Prefects Apostolic, IV-149 pp., 1924.
25. Correa, Rev. Jose Servelion, S.T.L., J.C.D., La Potestad Legislativa de la Iglesia Catolica, IV-127 pp., 1925.
26. Dugan, Rev. Henry Francis, A.M., J.C.D., The Judiciary Department of the Diocesan Curia, 87 pp., 1925.
27. Keller, Rev. Charles Frederick, S.T.B., J.C.D., Mass Stipends, 167 pp., 1925.
28. Paschang, Rev. John Linus, J.C.D., The Sacramentals According to the Code of Canon Law, 129 pp., 1925.
29. Piontek, Rev. Cyrillus, O.F.M., S.T.B., J.C.D., De Indulto Exclaustrationis necnon Saecularizationis, XIII-289 pp., 1925.
30. Kearney, Rev. Richard Joseph, S.T.B., J.C.D., Sponsors at Baptism According to the Code of Canon Law, IV-127 pp., 1925.
31. Bartlett, Rev. Chester Joseph, A.M., LL.B., J.C.D., The Tenure of Parochial Property in the United States of America, V-108 pp., 1926.
32. Kilker, Rev. Adrian Jerome, J.C.D., Extreme Unction, V-425 pp., 1926.
33. McCormick, Rev. Robert Emmett, J.C.D., Confessors of Religious, VIII-266 pp., 1926.
34. Miller, Rev. Newton Thomas, J.C.D., Founded Masses According to the Code of Canon Law, VII-93 pp., 1926.
35. Roelker, Rev. Edward G., S.T.D., J.C.D., Principles of Privilege According to the Code of Canon Law, XI-166 pp., 1926.
36. Bakalarczyk, Rev. Richardus, M.I.C., J.U.D., De Novitiatu, VIII-208 pp., 1927.
37. Pizzuti, Rev. Lawrence, O.F.M., J.U.L., De Parochis Religiosis, 1927. (Not Printed.)
38. Bliley, Rev. Nicholas Martin, O.S.B., J.C.D., Altars According to the Code of Canon Law, XIX-132 pp., 1927.
39. Brown, Mr. Brendan Francis, A.B., LL.M., J.U.D., The Canonical Juristic Personality with Special Reference to its Status in the United States of America, V-212 pp., 1927.

40. CAVANAUGH, REV. WILLIAM THOMAS, C.P., J.U.D., The Reservation of the Blessed Sacrament, VIII-101 pp., 1927.
41. DOHENY, REV. WILLIAM J., C.S.C., A.B., J.U.D., Church Property: Modes of Acquisition, X-118 pp., 1927.
42. FELDHAUS, REV. ALOYSIUS H., C.PP.S., J.C.D., Oratories, IX-141 pp., 1927.
43. KELLY, REV. JAMES PATRICK, A.B., J.C.D., The Jurisdiction of the Simple Confessor, X-208 pp., 1927.
44. NEUBERGER, REV. NICHOLAS J., J.C.D., Canon 6 or the Relation of the Codex Juris Canonici to the Preceding Legislation, V-95 pp., 1927.
45. O'KEEFE, REV. GERALD MICHAEL, J.C.D., Matrimonial Dispensations, Powers of Bishops, Priests, and Confessors, VIII-232 pp., 1927.
46. QUIGLEY, REV. JOSEPH A. M., A.B., J.C.D., Condemned Societies, 139 pp., 1927.
47. ZAPLOTNIK, REV. JOHANNES LEO, J.C.D., De Vicariis Foraneis, X-142 pp., 1927.
48. DUSKIE, REV. JOHN ALOYSIUS, A.B., J.C.D., The Canonical Status of the Orientals in the United States, VIII-196 pp., 1928.
49. HYLAND, REV. FRANCIS EDWARD, J.C.D., Excommunication, Its Nature, Historical Development and Effects, VIII-181 pp., 1928.
50. REINMANN, REV. GERALD JOSEPH, O.M.C., J.C.D., The Third Order Secular of Saint Francis, 201 pp., 1928.
51. SCHENK, REV. FRANCIS J., J.C.D., The Matrimonial Impediments of Mixed Religion and Disparity of Cult, XVI-318 pp., 1929.
52. COADY, REV. JOHN JOSEPH, S.T.D., J.U.D., A.M., The Appointment of Pastors, VIII-150 pp., 1929.
53. KAY, REV. THOMAS HENRY, J.C.D., Competence in Matrimonial Procedure, VIII-164 pp., 1929.
54. TURNER, REV. SIDNEY JOSEPH, C.P., J.U.D., The Vow of Poverty, XLIX-217 pp., 1929.
55. KEARNEY, REV. RAYMOND A., A.B., S.T.D., J.C.D., The Principles of Delegation, VII-149 pp., 1929.
56. CONRAN, REV. EDWARD JAMES, A.B., J.C.D., The Interdict, V-163 pp., 1930.
57. O'NEILL, REV. WILLIAM H., J.C.D., Papal Rescripts of Favor, VII-218 pp., 1930.
58. BASTNAGEL, REV. CLEMENT VINCENT, J.U.D., The Appointment of Parochial Adjutants and Assistants, XV-257 pp., 1930.
59. FERRY, REV. WILLIAM A., A.B., J.C.D., Stole Fees, V-136 pp., 1930.
60. COSTELLO, REV. JOHN MICHAEL, A.B., J.C.D., Domicile and Quasi-Domicile, VII-201 pp., 1930.
61. KREMER, REV. MICHAEL NICHOLAS, A.B., S.T.B., J.C.D., Church Support in the United States, VI-136 pp., 1930.
62. ANGULO, REV. LUIS, C.M., J.C.D., Legislation de la Iglesia sobre la intencion en la application de la Santa Misa, VII-104 pp., 1931.

63. Frey, Rev. Wolfgang Norbert, O.S.B., A.B., J.C.D., The Act of Religious Profession, VIII-174 pp., 1931.
64. Roberts, Rev. James Brendan, A.B., J.C.D., The Banns of Marriage, XIV-140 pp., 1931.
65. Ryder, Rev. Raymond Aloysius, A.B., J.C.D., Simony, IX-151 pp., 1931.
66. Campagna, Rev. Angelo, Ph.D., J.U.D., Il Vicario Generale del Vescovo, VII-205 pp., 1931.
67. Cox, Rev. Joseph Godfrey, A.B., J.C.D., The Administration of Seminaries, VI-124 pp., 1931.
68. Gregory, Rev. Donald J., J.U.D., The Pauline Privilege, XV-165 pp., 1931.
69. Donohue, Rev. John F., J.C.D., The Impediment of Crime, VII-110 pp., 1931.
70. Dooley, Rev. Eugene A., O.M.I., J.C.D., Church Law on Sacred Relics, IX-143 pp., 1931.
71. Orth, Rev. Clement Raymond, O.M.C., J.C.D., The Approbation of Religious Institutes, 171 pp., 1931.
72. Pernicone, Rev. Joseph M., A.B., J.C.D., The Ecclesiastical Prohibition of Books, XII-267 pp., 1932.
73. Clinton, Rev. Connell, A.B., J.C.D., The Paschal Precept, IX-108 pp., 1932.
74. Donnelly, Rev. Francis B., A.M., S.T.L., J.C.D., The Diocesan Synod, VIII-125 pp., 1932.
75. Torrente, Rev. Camilo, C.M.F., J.C.D., Las Procesiones Sagradas, V-145 pp., 1932.
76. Murphy, Rev. Edwin J., C.PP.S., J.C.D., Suspension Ex Informata Conscientia, XI-122 pp., 1932.
77. MacKenzie, Rev. Eric F., A.M., S.T.L., J.C.D., The Delict of Heresy in its Commission, Penalization, Absolution, VII-124 pp., 1932.
78. Lyons, Rev. Avitus E., S.T.B., J.C.D., The Collegiate Tribunal of First Instance, XI-147 pp., 1932.
79. Connolly, Rev. Thomas A., J.C.D., Appeals, XI-195 pp., 1932.
80. Sangmeister, Rev. Joseph V., A.B., J.C.D., Force and Fear as Precluding Matrimonial Consent, V-211 pp., 1932.
81. Jaeger, Rev. Leo A., A.B., J.C.D., The Administration of Vacant and Quasi-Vacant Episcopal Sees in the United States, IX-229 pp., 1932.
82. Rimlinger, Rev. Herbert T., J.C.D., Error Invalidating Matrimonial Consent, VII-79 pp., 1932.
83. Barrett, Rev. John D. M., S.S., J.C.D., A Comparative Study of the Third Plenary Council of Baltimore and the Code, IX-221 pp., 1932.
84. Carberry, Rev. John J., Ph.D., S.T.D., J.C.D., The Juridical Form of Marriage, X-177 pp., 1934.
85. Dolan, Rev. John L., A.B., J.C.D., The Defensor Vinculi, XII-157 pp., 1934.

86. HANNAN, REV. JEROME D., A.M., S.T.D., LL.B., J.C.D., The Canon Law of Wills, IX-517 pp., 1934.
87. LEMIEUX, REV. DELISE A., A.M., J.C.D., The Sentence in Ecclesiastical Procedure, IX-131 pp., 1934.
88. O'ROURKE, REV. JAMES J., A.B., J.C.D., Parish Registers, VII-109 pp., 1934.
89. TIMLIN, REV. BARTHOLOMEW, O.F.M., A.M., J.C.D., Conditional Matrimonial Consent, X-381 pp., 1934.
90. WAHL, REV. FRANCIS X., A.B., J.C.D., The Matrimonial Impediments of Consanguinity and Affinity, VI-125 pp., 1934.
91. WHITE, REV. ROBERT J., A.B., LL.B., S.T.B., J.C.D., Canonical Ante-Nuptial Promises and the Civil Law, VI-152 pp., 1934.
92. HERRERA, REV. ANTONIO PARRA, O.C.D., J.C.D., Legislacion Ecclesiastica sobra el Ayuno y la Abstinencia, XI-191 pp., 1935.
93. KENNEDY, REV. EDWIN J., J.C.D., The Special Matrimonial Process in Cases of Evident Nullity, X-165 pp., 1935.
94. MANNING, REV. JOHN J., A.B., J.C.D., Presumption of Law in Matrimonial Procedure, XI-111 pp., 1935.
95. MOEDER, REV. JOHN M., J.C.D., The Proper Bishop for Ordination and Dimissorial Letters, VII-135 pp., 1935.
96. O'MARA, REV. WILLIAM A., A.B., J.C.D., Canonical Causes for Matrimonial Dispensations, IX-155 pp., 1935.
97. REILLY, REV. PETER, J.C.D., Residence of Pastors, IX-81 pp., 1935.
98. SMITH, REV. MARINER T., O.P., S.T.Lr., J.C.D., The Penal Law for Religious, VII-169 pp., 1935.
99. WHALEN, REV. DONALD W., A.M., J.C.D., The Value of Testimonial Evidence in Matrimonial Procedure, XIII-297 pp., 1935.
100. CLEARY, REV. JOSEPH F., J.C.D., Canonical Limitations on the Alienation of Church Property, VIII-141 pp., 1936.
101. GLYNN, REV. JOHN C., J.C.D., The Promoter of Justice, XX-337 pp., 1936.
102. BRENNAN, REV. JAMES H., S.S., M.A., S.T.B., J.C.D., The Simple Convalidation of Marriage, VI-135 pp., 1937.
103. BRUNINI, REV. JOSEPH BERNARD, J.C.D., The Clerical Obligations of Canons 139 and 142, X-121 pp., 1937.
104. CONNOR, REV. MAURICE, A.B., J.C.D., The Administrative Removal of Pastors, VIII-159 pp., 1937.
105. GUILFOYLE, REV. MERLIN JOSEPH, J.C.D., Custom, XI-144 pp., 1937.
106. HUGHES, REV. JAMES AUSTIN, A.B., A.M., J.C.D., Witnesses in Criminal Trials of Clerics, IX-140 pp., 1937.
107. JANSEN, REV. RAYMOND J., A.B., S.T.L., J.C.D., Canonical Provisions for Catechetical Instruction, VII-153 pp., 1937.
108. KEALY, REV. JOHN JAMES, A.B., J.C.D., The Introductory Libellus in Church Court Procedure, XI-121 pp., 1937.

109. McMANUS, REV. JAMES EDWARD, C.SS.R., J.C.D., The Administration of Temporal Goods in Religious Institutes, XVI-196 pp., 1937.
110. MORIARTY, REV. EUGENE JAMES, J.C.D., Oaths in Ecclesiastical Courts, X-115 pp., 1937.
111. RAINER, REV. ELIGIUS GEORGE, C.SS.R., J.C.D., Suspension of Clerics, XVII-249 pp., 1937.
112. REILLY, REV. THOMAS F., C.SS.R., J.C.D., Visitation of Religious, VI-195 pp., 1938.
113. MORIARITY, REV. FRANCIS E., C.SS.R., J.C.D., The Extraordinary Absolution from Censures, XV-334 pp., 1938.
114. CONNOLLY, REV. NICHOLAS P., J.C.D., The Canonical Erection of Parishes, X-132 pp., 1938.
115. DONOVAN, REV. JAMES JOSEPH, J.C.D., The Pastor's Obligation in Prenuptial Investigation, XII-322 pp., 1938.
116. HARRIGAN, REV. ROBERT J., M.A., S.T.B., J.C.D., The Radical Sanation of Invalid Marriages, VIII-208 pp., 1938.
117. BOFFA, REV. CONRAD HUMBERT, J.C.D., Canonical Provisions for Catholic Schools, VII-211 pp., 1939.
118. PARSONS, REV. ANSCAR JOHN, O.M.Cap., J.C.D., Canonical Elections, XII-236 pp., 1939.
119. REILLY, REV. EDWARD MICHAEL, A.B., J.C.D., The General Norms of Dispensation, XII-156 pp., 1939.
120. RYAN, REV. GERALD ALOYSIUS, A.B., J.C.D., Principles of Episcopal Jurisdiction, XII-172 pp., 1939.
121. BURTON, REV. FRANCIS JAMES, C.S.C., A.B., J.C.D., A Commentary on Canon 1125, X-222 pp., 1940.
122. MIASKIEWICZ, REV. FRANCIS SIGISMUND, J.C.D., Supplied Jurisdiction According to Canon 209, XII-340 pp., 1940.
123. RICE, REV. PATRICK WILLIAM, A.B., J.C.D., Proof of Death in Prenuptial Investigation, VIII-156 pp., 1940.
124. ANGLIN, REV. THOMAS FRANCIS, M.S., J.C.D., The Eucharistic Fast, VIII-183 pp., 1941.
125. COLEMAN, REV. JOHN JEROME, J.C.D., The Minister of Confirmation, VI-153 pp., 1941.
126. DOWNS, REV. JOSEPH EMMANUEL, A.B., J.C.D., The Concept of Clerical Immunity, XI-163 pp., 1941.
127. ESSWEIN, REV. ANTHONY ALBERT, J.C.D., Extrajudicial Penal Powers of Ecclesiastical Superiors, X-144 pp., 1941.
128. FARRELL, REV. BENJAMIN FRANCIS, M.A., S.T.L., J.C.D., The Rights and Duties of the Local Ordinary Regarding Congregations of Women Religious of Pontifical Approval, V-195 pp., 1941.
129. FEENEY, REV. THOMAS JOHN, A.B., S.T.L., J.C.D., Restitutio in Integrum, VI-169 pp., 1941.
130. FINDLAY, REV. STEPHEN WILLIAM, O.S.B., A.B., J.C.D., Canonical

Norms Governing the Deposition and Degradation of Clerics, XVII-279 pp., 1941.

131. Goodwine, Rev. John, A.B., S.T.L., J.C.D., The Right of the Church to Acquire Property, VIII-119 pp., 1941.

132. Heston, Rev. Edward Louis, C.S.C., Ph.D., S.T.D., J.C.D., The Alienation of Church Property in the United States, XII-222 pp., 1941.

133. Hogan, Rev. James John, A.B., S.T.L., J.C.D., Judicial Advocates and Procurators, XIII-200 pp., 1941.

134. Kealy, Rev. Thomas M., A.B., Litt.B., J.C.D., Dowry of Women Religious, IX-152 pp., 1941.

135. Keene, Rev. Michael James, O.S.B., J.C.D., Religious Ordinaries and Canon 198, V-164 pp., 1942.

136. Kerin, Rev. Charles A., S.S., M.A., S.T.B., J.C.D., The Privation of Christian Burial, XVI-279 pp., 1941.

137. Louis, Rev. William Francis, M.A., J.C.D., Diocesan Archives, X-101 pp., 1941.

138. McDevitt, Rev. Gilbert Joseph, A.B., J.C.D., Legitimacy and Legitimation, X-247 pp., 1941.

139. McDonough, Rev. Thomas Joseph, A.B., J.C.D., Apostolic Administrators, X-217 pp., 1941.

140. Meier, Rev. Carl Anthony, A.B., J.C.D., Penal Administration Procedure Against Negligent Pastors, XI-240 pp., 1941.

141. Schmidt, Rev. John Rogg, A.B., J.C.D., The Principles of Authentic Interpretation in Canon 17 of the Code of Canon Law, XII-331 pp., 1941.

142. Slafkosky, Rev. Andrew Leonard, A.B., J.C.D., The Canonical Episcopal Visitation of the Diocese, X-197 pp., 1941.

143. Swoboda, Rev. Innocent Robert, O.F.M., J.C.D., Ignorance in Relation to the Imputability of Delicts, IX-271 pp., 1941.

144. Dubé, Rev. Arthur Joseph, A.B., J.C.D., The General Principles for the Reckoning of Time in Canon Law, VIII-299 pp., 1941.

145. McBride, Rev. James T., A.B., J.C.D., Incardination and Excardination of Seculars, XX-585 pp., 1941.

146 Król, Rev. John T., J.C.D., The Defendant in Ecclesiastical Trials, XII-207 pp., 1942.

147. Comyns, Rev. Joseph J., C.SS.R., A.B., J.C.D., Papal and Episcopal Administration of Church Property, XIV-155 pp., 1942.

148. Barry, Rev. Garrett Francis, O.M.I., J.C.D., Violation of the Cloister, XII-260 pp., 1942.

149. Bolduc, Rev. Gatien, C.S.V., A.B., S.T.L., J.C.D., Les Études dans les Religions Cléricales, VIII-155 pp., 1942.

150. Boyle, Rev. David John, M.A., J.C.D., The Juridic Effects of Moral Certitude on Pre-Nuptial Guarantees, XII-188 pp., 1942.

151. Canavan, Rev. Walter Joseph, M.A., Litt.D., J.C.D., The Profession of Faith, XII-143 pp., 1942.

152. DESROCHERS, REV. BRUNO, A.B., PH.L., S.T.B., J.C.D., Le Premier Concile Plénier de Québec et le Code de Droit Canonique, XIV–186 pp., 1942.

153. DILLON, REV. ROBERT EDWARD, A.B., J.C.D., Common Law Marriage, X-148 pp., 1942.

154. DODWELL, REV. EDWARD JOHN, PH.D., S.T.B., J.C.D., The Time and Place for the Celebration of Marriage, X-156 pp., 1942.

155. DONNELLAN, REV. THOMAS ANDREW, A.B., J.C.D., The Obligation of the Missa pro Populo, VII-131 pp., 1942.

156. ELTZ, REV. LOUIS ANTHONY, A.B., J.C.D., Cooperation in Crime, XII-208 pp., 1942.

157. GASS, REV. SYLVESTER FRANCIS, M.A., J.C.D., Ecclesiastical Pensions, XI-206 pp., 1942.

158. GUINIVEN, REV. JOHN JOSEPH, C.SS.R., J.C.D., The Precept of Hearing Mass, XIV-188 pp., 1942.

159. GULCZYNSKI, REV. JOHN THEOPHILUS, J.C.D., The Desecration and Violation of Churches, X-126 pp., 1942.

160. HAMMILL, REV. JOHN LEO, M.A., J.C.D., The Obligations of the Traveler According to Canon 14, VIII-204 pp., 1942.

161. HAYDT, REV. JOHN JOSEPH, A.B., J.C.D., Reserved Benefices, XI-148 pp., 1942.

162. HUSER, REV. ROGER JOHN, O.F.M., A.B., J.C.D., The Crime of Abortion in Canon Law, XII-187 pp., 1942.

163. KEARNEY, REV. FRANCIS PATRICK, A.B., S.T.L., J.C.L., The Principles of Canon 1127.

164. LINAHEN, REV. LEO JAMES, S.T.L., J.C.D., De Absolutione Complicis In Peccato Turpi, 114 pp., 1942.

165. MCCLOSKEY, REV. JOSEPH ALOYSIUS, A.B., J.C.D., The Subject of Ecclesiastical Law According to Canon 12, XVII-246 pp., 1942.

166. O'NEILL, REV. FRANCIS JOSEPH, C.SS.R., J.C.D., The Dismissal of Religious in Temporary Vows, XIII-220 pp., 1942.

167. PRINCE, REV. JOHN EDWARD, A.B., S.T.D., J.C.D., The Diocesan Chancellor, X-136 pp., 1942.

168. RIESNER, REV. ALBERT JOSEPH, C.SS.R., J.C.D., Apostates and Fugitives from Religious Institutes, IX-168 pp., 1942.

169. STENGER, REV. JOSEPH BERNARD, J.C.D., The Mortgaging of Church Property, 186 pp., 1942.

170. WALDRON, REV. JOSEPH FRANCIS, A.B., J.C.D., The Minister of Baptism, XII-197 pp., 1942.

171. WILLETT, REV. ROBERT ALBERT, J.C.D., The Probative Value of Documents in Ecclesiastical Trials, X-124 pp., 1942.

172. WOEBER, REV. EDWARD MARTIN, M.A., J.C.D., The Interpellations, XII-161 pp., 1942.

173. BENKO, REV. MATTHEW ALOYSIUS, O.S.B., M.A., J.C.D., The Abbot *Nullius*, XIV-148 pp., 1943.

174. Christ, Rev. Joseph James, M.A., S.T.L., J.C.D., Dispensation from Vindicative Penalties, XIV-285 pp., 1943.
175. Clancy, Rev. Patrick M. J., O.P., A.B., S.T.Lr., J.C.D., The Local Religious Superior, X-229 pp., 1943.
176. Clarke, Rev. Thomas James, J.C.D., Parish Societies, XII-147 pp., 1943.
177. Connolly, Rev. John Patrick, S.T.L., J.C.D., Synodal Examiners and Parish Priest Consultors, X-223 pp., 1943.
178. Drumm, Rev. William Martin, A.B., J.C.D., Hospital Chaplains, XII-175 pp., 1943.
179. Flanagan, Rev. Bernard Joseph, A.B., S.T.L., J.C.D., The Canonical Erection of Religious Houses, X-147 pp., 1943.
180. Kelleher, Rev. Stephen Joseph, A.B., S.T.B., J.C.D., Discussions with non-Catholics: Canonical Legislation, X-93 pp., 1943.
181. Lewis, Rev. Gordian, C.P., J.C.D., Chapters in Religious Institutes, XII-169 pp., 1943.
182. Marx, Rev. Adolph, J.C.D., The Declaration of Nullity of Marriages Contracted Outside the Church, X-151 pp., 1943.
183. Matulenas, Rev. Raymond Anthony, O.S.B., A.B., J.C.L., Communication, a Source of Privileges, XII-225 pp., 1943.
184. O'Leary, Rev. Charles Gerard, C.SS.R., J.C.D., Religious Dismissed After Perpetual Profession, X-213 pp., 1943.
185. Power, Rev. Cornelius Michael, J.C.D., The Blessing of Cemeteries, XII-231 pp., 1943.
186. Shuhler, Rev. Ralph Vincent, O.S.A., J.C.D., Privileges of Regulars to Absolve and Dispense, XII-195 pp., 1943.
187. Ziolkowski, Rev. Thaddeus Stanislaus, A.B., J.C.D., The Consecration and Blessing of Churches, XII-151 pp., 1943.
188. Heneghan, Rev. John Joseph, S.T.D., J.C.D., The Marriages of Unworthy Catholics: Canons 1065 and 1066, XVI-213 pp., 1944.
189. Carroll, Rev. Coleman Francis, M.A., S.T.L., J.C.L., Charitable Institutions.
190. Ciesluk, Rev. Joseph Edward, Ph.B., S.T.L., J.C.L., National Parishes in the United States.
191. Coburn, Rev. Vincent Paul, A.B., J.C.D., Marriages of Conscience, XII-172 pp., 1944.
192. Connors, Rev. Charles Paul, C.S.Sp., A.B., J.C.L., Extra-Judicial Procurators in the Code of Canon Law, X-94 pp., 1944.
193. Coyle, Rev. Paul Raymond, A.B., J.C.L., Judicial Exceptions.
194. Fair, Rev. Bartholomew Francis, A.B., S.T.L., J.C.L., The Impediment of Abduction.
195. Gallagher, Rev. Thomas Raphael, O.P., A.B., S.T.Lr., J.C.L., The Examination of the Qualities of the Ordinand, X-166 pp., 1944.
196. Gannon, Rev. John Mark, S.T.L., J.C.L., The Interstices Required for the Promotion to Orders, XII-100 pp., 1944.

197. Goldsmith, Rev. J. William, B.C.S., S.T.L., J.C.L., The Competence of Church and State over Marriage—Disputed Points, X-128 pp., 1944.
198. Goodwine, Rev. Joseph Gerard, A.B., S.T.B., J.C.L., The Reception of Converts, XIV-326 pp., 1944.
199. Kowalski, Rev. Romuald Eugene, O.F.M., A.B., J.C.D., Sustenance of Religious Houses of Regulars, X-174 pp., 1944.
200. McCoy, Rev. Alan Edward, O.F.M., J.C.D., Force and Fear in Relation to Delictual Imputability and Penal Responsibility, XII-160 pp., 1944.
201. McDevitt, Rev. Vincent John, Ph.B., S.T.L., J.C.L., Perjury.
202. Martin, Rev. Thomas Owen, Ph.D., S.T.D., J.C.D., Adverse Possession, Prescription and Limitation of Actions: The Canonical "Praescriptio," XX-208 pp., 1944.
203. Miklosovic, Rev. Paul John, A.B., J.C.L., Attempted Marriages and Their Consequent Juridic Effects.
204. Mundy, Rev. Thomas Maurice, A.B., S.T.L., J.C.L., The Union of Parishes.
205. O'Dea, Rev. John Coyle, A.B., J.C.D., The Matrimonial Impediment of Nonage, VIII-126 pp., 1944.
206. Olalia, Rev. Alexander Ayson, S.T.L., J.C.D., A Comparative Study of the Christian Constitution of States and the Constitution of the Philippine Commonwealth, XII, 136 pp., 1944.
207. Poisson, Rev. Pierre-Marie, C.S.C., A.B., Ph.L., Th.L., J.C.L., Droits Patrimoniaux des Maisons et des Églises Religieuses.
208. Stadalnikas, Rev. Casimir Joseph, M.I.C., J.C.D., Reservation of Censures, X-141 pp., 1944.
209. Sullivan, Rev. Eugene Henry, S.T.L., J.C.L., Proof of the Reception of the Sacraments.
210. Vaughan, Rev. William Edward, J.C.D., Constitutions for Diocesan Courts, X-210 pp., 1944.
211. Paro, Rev. Gino, S.T.D., J.C.L., The Right of Apostolic Delegation.
212. Balzer, Rev. Ralph Francis, C.P., J.C.L., The Computation of Time in a Canonical Novitiate.
213. Dougherty, Rev. John Whelan, A.B., S.T.L., J.C.L., De Inquisitione Speciali.
214. Dziob, Rev. Michael Walter, J.C.L., The Sacred Congregation for the Oriental Church.
215. Eidenschink, Rev. John Albert, O.S.B., B.A., J.C.L., The Election of Bishops in the Letters of Pope Gregory the Great.
216. Gill, Rev. Nicholas, C.P., J.C.L., The Spiritual Prefect in Clerical Religious Houses of Study.
217. Hynes, Rev. Harry Gerard, S.T.L., J.C.L., The Privileges of Cardinals.
218. McDevitt, Rev. Gerald Vincent, S.T.L., J.C.L., The Renunciation of an Ecclesiastical Office.

219. MANNING, REV. JOSEPH LEROY, J.C.L., The Free Conferral of Offices.
220. MEYER, REV. LOUIS G., O.S.B., A.B., S.T.B., J.C.L., Alms-Gathering by Religious.
221. O'DONNELL, REV. CLETUS FRANCIS, M.A., J.C.L., The Marriage of Minors.
222. PRUNSKIS, REV. JOSEPH, J.C.L., Comparative Law, Ecclesiastical and Civil, in Lithuanian Concordat.
223. SWEENEY, REV. FRANCIS PATRICK, C.Ss.R., J.C.L., The Reduction of Clerics to the Lay State.
224. VOGELPOHL, REV. HENRY JOHN, J.C.L., The Simple Impediments to Holy Orders.

www.ingramcontent.com/pod-product-compliance
Lightning Source LLC
LaVergne TN
LVHW050235080826
844660LV00012B/537

* 9 7 8 0 8 1 3 2 2 4 0 2 2 *